BEFORE THE BINDING OF THE BIBLICAL CANON

Scripture's Wider Collection Of Witnesses

R. R. David

Before The Binding Of The Biblical Canon

ISBN: 979-8-9952859-0-8

Cover design: R. R. David; Using KDP Cover Creator

Printed in the United States of America

Contact: r.r.david.author@gmail.com

PROLOGUE

The Court Of The Forgotten Witnesses

The chamber is vast and ancient, older than any earthly court yet strangely familiar. Its walls are lined with scrolls, some worn by centuries of use, others dimmed by long neglect. At the far end rises a great bench carved with the words of prophets and apostles

This is no court of men. This is the Courtroom of the Ancient Prophetic Witnesses.

A hush falls as the first scroll is called. Its voice is steady, speaking of the fathers, the covenant, and the God who remembers His people. Another rises, long dismissed and long silenced, yet echoing the same hope, pointing to visions and prophecy about the last generation. Then a third, then a fourth, once honored then hidden, each adding its voice to the same unfolding redemption.

For a time, what had been dismissed sounded like scattered solos is slowly gathering into a single rising harmony, as though these forgotten witnesses are finding their pitch again.

Then an objection. A modern scholar stands, armed with assumptions rather than scrolls. He questions their age, their absence from lists, what other men determined about them, their worthiness.

The court grows still.

The Judge speaks with firm truth. "Were these witnesses rejected because they lied . . . or because men forgot how to listen?"

Silence.

One by one the witnesses step forward again, their testimonies aligning like a choir around the central melody of Scripture. They speak of righteousness, mercy, covenant, repentance, hope, and the God who does not change who in His mercy provided a new covenant when the first was broken.

The Judge declares, "Let the record show that these witnesses were never disqualified by Me. Their testimonies stand."

The gavel falls.

The hearing ends.

But the invitation remains:

Will the people of this generation listen to the testimonies of the witnesses who were silenced by men . . . or only to the men who silenced the witnesses?

✦✧✦

TABLE OF CONTENTS

INTRODUCTION
The Beginning Of The Ancient Path

How Revelation Was Given And Preserved Through The Prophets' And Apostles' Writings And Made Its Way to Believers Today

"And the generations shall know My words, for I have given them to the righteous to declare forever." – 1 Enoch 82:1

"These things I command you to write and preserve for the generations of the world." – Jubilees 1:26

"He established a testimony in Jacob, and appointed a law in Israel, which he commanded our fathers, that they should make them known to their children: that the generation to come might know them." – Psalm 78:5-6

"As for me, this is my covenant with them, saith the Lord (יהוה/Yahweh); My spirit that is upon thee, and my words which I have put in thy mouth,
shall not depart out of thy mouth, nor out of the mouth of thy seed, nor out of the mouth of thy seed's seed, saith the Lord (יהוה/Yahweh), from henceforth and for ever." – Isaiah 59:21

"For the Highest hath revealed many secret things unto thee, and hath shown thee the deep things of the times." – 2 Esdras 14:5

The Ancient Path, rooted in the earliest Scriptural history, offers insight into how covenant, wisdom, and divine instruction were understood across generations. From the beginning, *יהוה/Yahweh* spoke into the world He made and entrusted His words to those who would carry them. Prophets proclaimed them, scribes recorded them, and elders guarded them so each generation might receive what had been given before. Along this ancient path, revelation moved from voice to memory, from memory to writing, and from writing to the guardians who preserved it.

Why This Book Begins Somewhere Different

For generations, Christians have inherited a familiar story about how the Bible came to be. It is a story told in seminary classrooms, church pamphlets, apologetics books, and countless online articles. The details vary, but the broad outline is the same: Israel recognized the Law, The Prophets, and The Writings; the early assemblies received the apostolic gospels, epistle and Revelation; councils later confirmed what had been assumed that God had already made clear. The canon, we are told, is trustworthy because the right criteria were used – prophetic or apostolic authorship, doctrinal consistency, widespread use, and the Spirit's guidance of God's people in setting its boundaries.

There is much in this story that is honorable. It reflects a genuine desire to safeguard the Scriptures, to preserve the words that have shaped the faith of millions – maybe billions – and to resist the chaos of every new sermon, study, video or writing claiming divine authority to define how the canon came to be. These accounts rightly emphasize that God speaks through chosen witnesses, and that His people have long sought to discern those voices with care. They remind us that the canon did not fall from the sky but emerged through history, devotion, and discernment.

Yet these same narratives share a quiet assumption: that the prophetic witness is fully contained within the modern official list. They focus on the boundaries of the binding rather than the breadth of the testimony. They acknowledge – briefly, almost reluctantly – that the prophets and apostles referenced other writings, cited other texts, and drew from a wider body of material than what appears between our Bibles' covers.

The prophets are allowed to point to these works, but the works themselves are rarely allowed to speak.

This book takes the next, braver step. Instead of beginning with "the list" and the history of how it came to be, it begins with the prophets themselves – the very men whose words form the foundation of the canon. If we already trust patriarchs and prophets such as Abraham, Moses, Samuel, Nathan, Gad, David, Isaiah, Jeremiah, Ezekiel, Daniel, and look to the apostles as God's chosen witnesses, then it is worth asking what else they wrote, referenced, or preserved. Scripture itself tells us that their testimonies extended beyond the pages we now call "canonical." The question is not whether we should expand the Bible, but whether we have been willing to hear the full prophetic chorus that the Bible itself acknowledges.

This work does not chase every lost or legendary text. It follows the trail the prophets left inside the canon – citations, allusions, and explicit references to other writings by the same trusted voices named in the canonical narrative. It invites readers to consider that God's revelation was not confined to a later fixed list but expressed through a living, interconnected prophetic tradition and history. The goal is not to unsettle faith but to deepen it, not to challenge Scripture but to honor the fullness of the prophetic witness that Scripture itself affirms.

In short: this book moves the conversation from defending the canon to listening to the prophets. And when we do, we discover that the story of God's revelation is wider, richer, and more coherent than the boundaries of the binding have allowed us to see.

Why Hebrew Stands at the Foundation, Not Greek Alone

Although Greek became the *lingua franca* of the era – the widely shared common tongue used across the Mediterranean region for communication among diverse peoples – following the conquests of Alexander the *Great*, the spread of a common trade language does not determine the language in which the revelation of יהוה/*Yahweh* first appeared.

The Gospel was proclaimed first to the house of Israel, and the earliest witnesses lived, taught, and worshiped within a Hebrew-speaking world. Increasing evidence from linguistic patterns, Semitic idioms, Hebraic parallelism, and early testimony suggests that many apostolic writings originated in Hebrew and were later translated into Greek to reach Gentile, non-Hebrew speaking peoples. As the generations passed, fewer believers were taught in Hebrew, spoke Hebrew, or read the Hebrew Scriptures, and the Greek translations naturally became the versions most widely copied and circulated. This linguistic reality is reflected in the inscription Pilate ordered to be placed above יֵשׁוּעַ/Yeshua during his crucifixion, written in Hebrew, Latin, and Greek:

> *"This title then read many of the Jews: for the place where Jesus was crucified was nigh to the city: and it was written in Hebrew, and Greek, and Latin." – John 19:20 (See also Matthew 27:37; Mark 15:26; Luke 23:38).*

Pilate's inscription would have been written as:

Hebrew – ישוע הנצרי מלך היהודים

Latin – IESVS NAZARENVS REX IVDAEORVM

Greek – Ἰησοῦς ὁ Ναζωραῖος ὁ βασιλεὺς τῶν Ἰουδαίων.

The first-century writing about יֵשׁוּעַ/Yeshua's trial, sentencing, crucifixion and resurrection contained in the compilation called *Acts of Pilate/Gospel of Nicodemus* also portrays Pilate as unable to follow the speech of the Jewish leaders, repeatedly requiring clarification of their accusations, which reflects the historical reality that Roman officials in Judea spoke **Latin** and did not speak **Hebrew** and relied on interpreters when dealing with the Sanhedrin. **Greek** served as the vehicle for wider transmission, but the substance, worldview, and internal logic of the writings reflect a **Hebrew** foundation. Recognizing this distinction does not diminish the value of the Greek manuscripts; it simply restores the historical reality that revelation was first spoken in **Hebrew** – the language of the covenant people before being rendered into the *lingua franca* for the sake of the nations.

The Divine Hebrew Names Used Throughout This Book

This book uses the Hebrew form of the Name of the Creator and Heavenly Father, and of His Beloved Son, the Messiah and Savior. In most Hebrew manuscripts from the post-exilic period onward, *יהוה* (Yahweh – pronounced YAH-weh) appears in the square Hebrew script, replacing the much older Paleo-Hebrew Divine Name used in some of the Dead Sea Scrolls and other ancient Hebrew inscriptions. יהוה/*Yahweh* consists of the letters (י) "Yod", (ה) "Hey", (ו) "Vav", and another (ה) "Hey".

In this book, the Messiah's name is written as יֵשׁוּעַ (Yeshua – pronounced *yeh-SHOO-ah).* Yeshua is the shortened post-exilic form of יְהוֹשֻׁעַ (Yehoshua – pronounced yeh-HO-shoo-ah), meaning " יהוה/Yahweh is salvation." יֵשׁוּעַ/Yeshua consists of the letters (י) Yod, (שׁ) Shin, (וּ) Vav, and (ע) Ayin.

This choice to use the square script Hebrew forms of the Divine Names of Father as יהוה/Yahweh and His Son as יֵשׁוּעַ/Yeshua – is made with respect for the diversity of traditions among readers and with the hope of avoiding unnecessary barriers and controversy. By using the Hebrew forms of the Names in most places where "God", "Lord", "Lord God", "Jesus", "Jesus Christ", "Christ" or "Christ Jesus" – apart from direct quotations or citations – this book simply adopts and uses the most historically universal Hebrew representations of the Divine Names found across the ancient manuscripts themselves, allowing the focus to remain on the message rather than on differing conventions or preferences. Because readers come from many communities with deeply held views about how these Names should be pronounced, this book does not attempt to resolve those debates and controversies; the forms used here serve only as familiar and accessible renderings for print and audio formats, so that attention may remain on the prophetic and apostolic witness these ancient and historic writings preserve.

Wisdom and Discernment Concerning Extracanonical Writings

It is understood that not every ancient writing claiming Scriptural authenticity should be received as edifying or as bearing genuine prophetic testimony. Ultimately, texts that are Divinely inspired and authored by Divinely appointed prophets and apostles – together with those preserved and transmitted by apostle-approved, Spirit-led overseers of the assemblies – must still be discerned by each individual believer – for Judgment Day concerns the individual, who will stand before the Almighty without the shelter of pastoral influence or any form of 'pastoral immunity.'

In gathering these ancient witnesses at the outset, this chapter restores a truth spoken from the beginning: every soul stands personally accountable before יהוה/Yahweh, and every action or practice – whether good or evil – comes under His judgment. These passages are placed here not as ornament, but as orientation. They remind the reader that the words preserved in Scripture and in the writings of the elders were never meant to be received secondhand or untested. They call each person to hear, to weigh, and to discern for themselves the path that leads to eternal Life. Before any discussion of lost or missing books, disputed texts, or forgotten voices, the foundation must be laid: יהוה/Yahweh judges with perfect equity, and every soul must seek His truth with fear, humility, and integrity.

The Witness of the Early Prophets

> *"Also unto thee, O Lord, belongeth mercy: for thou renderest to every man according to his work." – Psalm 62:12*
>
> *"If thou sayest, Behold, we knew it not; doth not he that pondereth the heart consider it? and he that keepeth thy soul, doth not he know it? and shall not he render to every man according to his works?" – Proverbs 24:12*
>
> *"For the work of a man shall he render unto him, and cause every man to find according to his ways." – Job 34:11*

"I the Lord search the heart, I try the reins, even to give every man according to his ways, and according to the fruit of his doings." – Jeremiah 17:10

"Great in counsel, and mighty in work: for thine eyes are open upon all the ways of the sons of men: to give every one according to his ways, and according to the fruit of his doings." – Jeremiah 32:19

"For God shall bring every work into judgment, with every secret thing, whether it be good, or whether it be evil." – Ecclesiastes 12:14

"For though Adam first sinned and brought untimely death upon all, yet of those who were born from him each one has prepared for his own soul the coming torment." – 2 Baruch 54:19 (R. H. Charles 1896 translation)

The Witness Of The Messiah And Apostles

"For the Son of man shall come in the glory of his Father with his angels; and then he shall reward every man according to his works." – Matthew, Gospel of Matthew 16:27

"Who will render to every man according to his deeds." – Paul, Letter to the Romans 2:6

"For we must all appear before the judgment seat of Christ; that every one may receive the things done in his body, according to that he hath done, whether it be good or bad." – Paul, 2 Corinthians 5:10

"And if ye call on the Father, who without respect of persons judgeth according to every man's work, pass the time of your sojourning here in fear." – Peter, First Letter of Peter 1:17

"And all the churches shall know that I am he which searcheth the reins and hearts: and I will give unto every one of you according to your works." – Spoken by יֵשׁוּעַ*/Yeshua, recorded by John's pen in Revelation 2:23*

"And the dead were judged out of those things which were written in the books, according to their works." – John, Revelation 20:12–13

"And, behold, I come quickly; and my reward is with me, to give every man according as his work shall be." – Spoken by יֵשׁוּעַ*/Yeshua, recorded by John, Revelation 22:12*

Discerning Truth

There are many Gnostic writings that fail apostolic scrutiny, and there are also many true writings that are falsely regarded as Gnostic. Those true teachings easily pass apostolic scrutiny and run parallel to the apostolic witness. But because of philosophical and doctrinal bias, many beneficial writings have been and remain disapproved of and heaped together with pseudo- and Gnostic writings, hence believers are directed to *'throw the baby out with the bathwater'*.

It is worth noting, without going further than this book intends, that the history of Scripture transmission has often intersected with political and religious power. From Ptolemy's commissioning of the Septuagint to Constantine's magnificent Greek Bibles, to Damasus' Latin Vulgate, and later royal projects such as the King James Bible, rulers and church leaders have repeatedly sponsored the production of Scripture for purposes that were not always purely devotional. Some of these early codices – large, ornate, and costly – seem to have vanished, while others may rest quietly in prestigious libraries and collections across the world. This book does not attempt to explore those larger motivations but simply invites the reader to notice the pattern and consider how such forces may have shaped which writings were preserved, which were set aside, and how the wider prophetic witness of early believers came to be narrowed in later centuries.

Revelation Before the Canon

Long before there was a canon, יהוה/Yahweh's ways were already being made known. Revelation lived in the lives and memories of those who walked with Him. Truth was preserved through faithful transmission – prophets recording what they had seen, priests safeguarding what had been entrusted to them, elders guiding the young, parents instructing children. Recognizing that revelation predates canon does not diminish Scriptural veracity; it simply acknowledges that ' יהוה/Yahweh spoke long before any formal collection of writings existed.

Scripture affirms that revelation was spoken, written, rehearsed, and carried forward through the generations. The endurance of truth rested upon faithful generational teaching. To depart from that revelation proved perilous.

> *"And also all that generation were gathered unto their fathers and there arose another generation after them, which knew not the Lord, nor yet the works which he had done for Israel." – Judges 2:10*

Prophetic Books Beyond the Boundaries of the Canon

Scripture references prophetic and historical writings that were known, preserved, and circulated among יהוה/Yahweh's people but were not included in the later decisions that formed canon. Joshua cites *Jasher* (*Joshua* 10:13; *2 Samuel* 1:18); *Chronicles* mentions the chronicles, books and records of Samuel, Nathan, and Gad (*1 Chronicles* 29:29; *2 Chronicles* 9:29; 12:15); *Jude* quotes *1 Enoch* (*Jude* 14–15); Paul instructs assemblies to read his first letter to the Corinthians and his letter to the Laodiceans (*1 Corinthians* 5:9; *Colossians* 4:16). These works were included and functionally present in the assemblies' ancient prophetic and Messianic apostolic narrative and literary world but are now extremely difficult to find.

In the time of Jesus, Jewish leaders were fully aware of a much wider body of sacred writings than the later canon would contain, works such as *Enoch, Jubilees*, the *Testaments of the Twelve Patriarchs*, and visionary texts like the *Vision/Ascension of Isaiah.* These writings circulated broadly and were copied, preserved, and respected, yet only the Torah, the Prophets, and the Writings were treated as authoritative Scripture. The Torah consists of *Genesis, Exodus, Leviticus, Numbers,* and *Deuteronomy.* The Prophets include *Isaiah, Jeremiah, Ezekiel, Daniel, Hosea, Jonah, Micah, Zechariah,* and *Malachi.* The Writings include *Psalms, Proverbs, Job,* and *Chronicles.*

The rest of the writings were placed in a category of revered literature that was known but not publicly taught. This selective emphasis created a form of gatekeeping, for by narrowing which texts were read, discussed, or interpreted in the synagogue, the leaders shaped how the people understood יהוה/Yahweh, His coming Messiah, and the Kingdom.

"You shut up the kingdom of heaven before men; you do not enter yourselves, and those who are entering you hinder." ׳ישׁוּע/Yeshua, Matthew 23:13

ישׁוּע/Yeshua's critique of the Pharisees, saying they did not "enter" and hindered others, fits this long-standing pattern in which access to the fullness of Israel's literary and prophetic heritage was limited. Over time, this same dynamic influenced how "canon" was defined, how collections and Bibles were formed, and how teaching and doctrine developed from reliance upon these narrowed collections, leaving a lasting imprint on interpretation down to the present day.

Dead Sea Scrolls Discovery in the 1940's

The texts discovered within the Dead Sea Scrolls confirmed that ancient Israel preserved a wide range of prophetic, historical, and wisdom texts, including works attributed to Enoch, Noah, Abraham, Jacob's twelve sons, Moses, and others. These manuscripts show that ancient Israel maintained a rich library of writings long before any later canon was defined.

The gathered and collected writings of the apostolic age populated the atmosphere surrounding the early assemblies. Influenced by the urgency to establish themselves as the divinely appointed curators and final authority of the Church, early councils ignored the existence of and reference to additional writings and quickly finalized the official canon. The appearance of a political maneuver would seem to have influenced the finalization and binding of the modern canonical collection.

How Revelation Has Moved Through Generations

The prophets who followed Enoch did not introduce new messages, but each generation preserved what יהוה/Yahweh had revealed from the beginning. This movement of prophetic revelation is evidence of why Scripture speaks of a more detailed record of the beginning called *"the Book of the generations of Adam"*. Prophets wrote visions, and priests safeguarded sacred records.

The opening chapter of this volume presents the foundation for the entire book – how יהוה/Yahweh spoke, how Divine revelation began, how it was preserved, and why prophetic writings beyond the later canonical limitations matter. With the groundwork in place, the remaining chapters move swiftly, each focusing on a single prophetic witness (with the exception of the chapter on the apostles) and each chapter concludes with a follow-up *Two-Fold Witness* section – showing how a given writing both affirms and confirms other prophetic works and is then affirmed and confirmed by other prophetic authors. This allows the reader to weigh each text responsibly, recognizing what is trustworthy, what may be questionable, and what meaningfully aligns with the broader Scriptural prophetic witness.

This book invites the reader to rediscover how revelation moved through יהוה/Yahweh's prophets and to His scribes for all generations to follow. Here readers encounter the writings that shaped early faith of יהוה/Yahweh's people, guided the first believers, and preserved what had been received.

And now we turn to the journey itself, walking through the lesser-known prophetic and apostolic writings revered by ancient Hebrew-speaking Israel and treasured by the early assemblies of יֵשׁוּעַ/Yeshua's followers.

Though many more extracanonical material was produced by the patriarchs and prophets, this book explores the following notable texts:

Ancient Hebrew Writings:

- *1 Enoch*
- *Jubilees*
- *Jasher*
- *Testament of Abraham*
- *Testament of Isaac*
- *Testament of Jacob (Israel)*
- *Testaments of the Twelve Patriarchs*
- *Apocalypse/Apocryphon of Abraham*

- *1 and 2 Baruch*
- *1 Esdras (4 Ezra & 2 Esdras)*
- *Psalms of Solomon*
- *Wisdom of Solomon*
- *Sirach (Ecclesiasticus)*
- *1-2 and 4 Maccabees*
- *Book of Gad the Seer*
- *Vision/Ascension of Isaiah*
- *Selected Dead Sea Scrolls texts and fragments*

Apostolic Writings Associated With The Apostles And The Early Bishops:

- *The Didache*
- *Acts of the Apostles*
- *Protoevangelium of James*
- *History of Joseph the Carpenter*
- *Epistle of Barnabas*
- *Gospel of Nicodemus/Acts of Pilate*
- *Letters of Ignatius of Antioch*
- *Epistle of Polycarp to the Philippians*
- *1 and 2 Clement*
- *Against Heresies by Irenaeus of Lyons*
- *The Shepherd of Hermas*

See the "Recommended Reading Lists" in the After Matter of this book.

THE FIRST ERA:
Before The Flood

Enoch

The Prophet Who Walked With God And Saw The Coming Judgment

"Enoch walked with God; then he was not, for God took him." – Genesis 5:24

"And behold! He cometh with ten thousands of His holy ones to execute judgment upon all, and to destroy all the ungodly: and to convict all flesh of all the works of the ungodliness which they have ungodly committed, and of all the hard things which ungodly sinners have spoken against Him." – 1 Enoch 1:9

"And Enoch also, the seventh from Adam, prophesied of these, saying, Behold, the Lord cometh with ten thousands of his saints, To execute judgment upon all, and to convince all that are ungodly among them of all their ungodly deeds which they have ungodly committed, and of all their hard speeches which ungodly sinners have spoken against him." – Jude 14-15 (quote of 1 Enoch 1:9)

"And go, say to the Watchers of heaven . . . 'And therefore I have not appointed wives for you; for the spiritual beings of heaven, in heaven is their dwelling.'" – 1 Enoch 15:2-7

"Ye do err, not knowing the Scriptures, nor the power of God. For in the resurrection they neither marry, nor are given in marriage, but are as the angels of God in heaven." – Matthew 22:29-30 quoting 1 Enoch 15:2-7

"By faith Enoch was translated that he should not see death; and was not found, because God had translated him: for before his translation he had this testimony, that he pleased God." Hebrews 11:5 (reference to 1 Enoch 12:1 and Jubilees 10:17)

The Book of 1 Enoch, attributed to the prophet and patriarch Enoch, the son of Jared, great grandfather of Noah – offers prophetic insight into divine judgment and the mysteries of the heavenly realm, preserved in early Hebrew collections within the Dead Sea Scrolls.

1. Enoch - A Scribe, Patriarch and Prophet

Enoch is presented as the first prophet and scribe, the first to ascend into the presence of the Most High. *Jubilees* describes him as the one who learned writing, recorded heavenly signs, and wrote a testimony for all generations (*Jubilees* 4:17–19). His son Methuselah and great-grandson Noah continued this scribal line, preserving and transmitting what Enoch saw (*1 Enoch* 82:1–2; 106:13–17). Noah entrusted these writings to Shem (*Jubilees* 10:12–14; 21:10; *Jasher* 3), who safeguarded them after the flood. The presence of multiple hands in *1 Enoch* mirrors the composite nature of works like *Psalms* and *Proverbs.*

2. Writings Attributed to Enoch

1 Enoch stands at the head of the earliest prophetic writings. In its original Hebrew and Aramaic setting, it was known as an *apocryphon* – a preserved writing safeguarded for the wise and for a future generation. Early Israel and the apostolic assemblies treated *1 Enoch* as Scripture, reading it alongside the law and prophets. The Ethiopian Bible still preserves it as Scripture.

1 Enoch goes into more detail about the beginning filling in what *Genesis* only outlines. For example where *Genesis* leaves much room for speculation regarding "the sons of God went into the daughters of men and begat giants", *1 Enoch* states clearly what historically occurred leaving little to speculation. *1 Enoch* contains the prophetic content that later prophets expound upon including themes reflected in the *Book of Revelation* regarding the very last of days.

3. Authentication of *1 Enoch*

The ancient testimony surrounding *1 Enoch* affirms its authenticity and reveals how it was preserved within Israel's prophetic heritage. The canonical books preserve only brief echoes of Enoch's story, yet *Genesis, Hebrews, 2 Peter,* and *Jude* – all reference or quote Enochic material.

Qumran fragments of *1 Enoch* confirm that Enochic writings circulated in distinct parts, later gathered under Enoch's name because they preserved his visions and the testimony of his descendants.

Jubilees and *Jasher* describe Enoch as the first scribe who recorded heavenly wisdom for future generations. These ancient witnesses affirm that *1 Enoch* was known, copied, and valued across the centuries.

> *"The Book of Enoch… is regarded as sacred by many, though not included in the canon." – Eusebius, Ecclesiastical History 6.25.1–2*

The Aramaic fragments discovered at Qumran confirm that multiple sections of *1 Enoch* – the *Book of the Watchers*, the *Astronomical Book*, and *Dream Visions* – circulated long before the time of יֵשׁוּעַ/Yeshua. Eleven manuscripts of *1 Enoch* were found near the Dead Sea in the caves of Qumran between 1947 and 1956, making it among one of the most numerous of the discovered books in the Dead Sea Scrolls. Alongside it, fifteen manuscripts of *Jubilees,* twenty-three of *Genesis,* thirty-three of *Deuteronomy,* thirty-six of *Psalms* and twenty-one of the *Book of Isaiah* demonstrate that the Enoch and *Jubilees* manuscripts stood within the heart of Israel's prophetic worldview and were preserved with the same reverence as all other old testament scrolls.

Historical Testimony

The historical testimony concerning *1 Enoch* is reflected in the following ancient sources, which bear witness to its reception and use:

> *"We may indeed accept the Book of Enoch, not as having been admitted into the Jewish canon, but as having been published before the deluge by Enoch himself." – Tertullian, On the Apparel of Women 3.3*

> *"The book of Enoch, which is not received in the canon, is nevertheless used by many in the Church." – Origen, Commentary on Matthew 10.23*

> *"Some have not inappropriately judged that the words of Enoch, which are quoted by the Apostle Jude, are taken from a certain apocryphal book." –*

Augustine, City of God 15.23

4. Value of *1 Enoch* to Modern Readers

To understand the world of the prophets and apostles, readers must hear Enoch's voice for themselves. *1 Enoch* removes barriers to understanding the earliest Scriptural history and invites readers into the same ancient hope that directed Israel all the way forward to the followers of **יֵשׁוּעַ**/Yeshua.

———— ✦✧✦ ————

TWO-FOLD WITNESS:
HOW *1 ENOCH* AFFIRMS AND IS AFFIRMED BY OTHER PROPHETIC WITNESSES

Essential Content From *1 Enoch* Paralleling Biblical Authors

- The Watchers and the origin of corruption: *Genesis 6*; *2 Peter 2:4–5; Jude 6*.
- The *Vision of Weeks*: *1 Enoch* 93:1–10; 91:12–17 provides the earliest prophetic timeline later echoed by:
- *Testament of Levi*: 2:1–3; 4:1; 5:1; 14:1–4; 16:1–5; 18:2
- *Jeremiah*: 25:11–12; 29:10
- *Daniel*: 9:2, 24–27
- *Revelation*: 11:2–3; 12:6, 14; 13:5; 20:4–6
- Judgment of the wicked and vindication of the righteous deepen Biblical themes found in *Matthew 25* and *Revelation 20*.

Additional Ancient Writings Confirm These Themes

- *Jubilees*: angelic rebellion, early chronology, heavenly tablets
- Testaments of the Twelve Patriarchs: shared prophetic themes
- *Book of the Watchers* traditions in the Dead Sea Scrolls: angelic rebellion, judgment, heavenly tablets
- *Book of The Giants*: Watcher offspring, judgment, heavenly visions
- *Testament of Levi*: heavenly ascent, priestly revelation, angelic mediation
- *Testament of Naphtali*: cosmic order, angelic roles, divine oversight
- *Ecclesiasticus/Sirach*: praise of ancient prophets, transmission of wisdom
- *Wisdom of Solomon*: righteous judgment, vindication of the faithful, cosmic justice

New Testament Writings Resonating With Enoch's Prophecies

- *Matthew 24–25*: angels, separation of righteous and wicked, judgment
- *Luke 17*: days of Noah as a paradigm for final judgment
- *John 5*: the Son of Man as judge of the living and the dead
- *Acts 7*: angelic mediation and divine oversight.
- *Romans 2*: impartial judgment and accountability

- *1 Corinthians 6*: saints judging angels.
- *2 Peter 2* and *Jude 6, 14–15*: direct use of Enochic themes
- *Revelation 1, 14, 20*: heavenly books, judgment scenes, vindication of the righteous.

SECOND ERA: After The Flood

Noah

His Voice And Influence Throughout The Generations

"Noah was a righteous man, blameless among his generations; Noah walked with God." – Genesis 6:9(b)

"And Noah found grace and righteousness before the Lord, for he was humble in all his deeds." – Jasher 5:13

"Noah was perfect in righteousness; therefore the Lord revealed to him what was coming upon the earth." – Jubilees 10:17

"For thus Enoch, the father of your father Methuselah, commanded his son, and Methuselah his son commanded his son Lamech, and Lamech commanded me [Noah] all the things which his fathers commanded him." – Jubilees 7:38-39

"[God] spared not the old world, but saved Noah the eighth person, a preacher of righteousness." – 2 Peter 2:5

"By faith Noah, being warned of God of things not seen as yet, moved with fear, prepared an ark to the saving of his house; by the which he condemned the world, and became heir of the righteousness which is by faith." – Hebrews 11:7

The writings associated with Noah remembered by ancient Israel and the followers of יֵשׁוּעַ/Yeshua offer themes of post-flood renewal, righteousness, preservation, and how God's dealings with humanity continued after the flood.

1. Noah As Patriarch, Prophet, Scribe and Teacher

Ancient testimony presents Noah as far more than the builder of the ark. *Genesis* portrays Noah as righteous, blameless, walking with יהוה/Yahweh, receiving divine commandments, offering pure sacrifices, and transmitting covenantal instruction to his sons. Early Jewish writings expand this portrait, remembering Noah as a scribe, a teacher, and a preserver of the earliest revelations.

> *"Noah was a righteous man, blameless among his generations; Noah walked with God." – Genesis 6:9(b)*

Jubilees (by Moses) describes Noah instructing his sons in "the commandments and the judgments and the ordinances" entrusted to him.

> *"And in the twenty-eighth jubilee Noah began to enjoin upon his sons' sons the ordinances and commandments, and all the judgments that he knew…" Jubilees 7:20–21*

Jubilees further records that the angels of the presence taught Noah the remedies needed to counteract the corruption of the Watchers, and that Noah wrote down all things in a book as he was instructed. He then entrusted this writing to Shem, ensuring that the wisdom of the old world did not perish in the Flood.

> *"And Noah wrote down all things in a book as we instructed him concerning every kind of medicine. Thus the evil spirits were precluded from hurting the sons of Noah. And he gave all that he had written to Shem, his eldest son; for he loved him exceedingly above all his sons." – Jubilees 10:13–14*

Jasher records Noah warning them against the sins that brought the Flood. These teachings included warnings against violence, fornication, and the corruption introduced by the Watchers.

> *"And Noah and Methuselah spoke all the words of the Lord to the sons of men, day after day, constantly speaking to them. But the sons of men would not hearken to them, nor incline their ears to their words, and they were stiff-necked. And the Lord granted them a period of one hundred and twenty years, saying, If they will return, then will God repent of the evil, so as not to destroy the earth." – Jasher 5:8-10 (see 5:6-12)*

Noah stands at the threshold between two worlds; the last righteous heir of the antediluvian/pre-flood age and the first post-flood scribe whose teachings guided the earliest generations. His 950-year lifespan allowed him to inherit the full weight of antediluvian wisdom and ensure it was passed down to future generations.

The Enochic tradition preserves the line of transmission that preceded him. Enoch entrusted his revelations to his son Methuselah, who passed them to Lamech, who in turn passed them to Noah.

> *"Enoch commanded his son Methuselah, and Methuselah his son Lamech, and Lamech commanded me [Noah] all the things which his fathers had commanded him." – Jubilees 7:38–39*

Several passages in *1 Enoch* (chapters 60; 65–67; 106–107) depict Noah receiving visions, warnings, and prophetic instruction that originated with Enoch himself. *Jubilees* summarizes Noah's role and legacy:

> *"And Noah wrote down all things in a book as we instructed him concerning every kind of medicine. Thus the evil spirits were precluded from hurting the sons of Noah. And he gave all that he had written to Shem, his eldest son; for he loved him exceedingly above all his sons. . . . And in his life on earth he excelled the children of men save Enoch because of the righteousness wherein he was perfect. For Enoch's office was ordained for a testimony to the generations of the world, so that he should recount all the deeds of generation unto generation till the day of judgment." – Jubilees 10:13–17*

Shem emerges from this inheritance as the custodian of the ancient records. Though Scripture speaks of him briefly, ancient writings remember him as a priestly figure, a keeper of genealogies, a witness to the covenant, and a teacher of righteousness. *Jasher* preserves the remembrance that Abram spent his early years learning in the house of Noah and Shem. Through this lineage, the earliest revelations flowed into the life of Abraham, forming the spiritual foundation of the patriarchal era.

In these writings, Noah preserved the teachings; Shem guarded them; Eber transmitted them; Abraham restored them; Isaac and Jacob inherited them; and Levi and his descendants safeguarded them. This lineage forms the backbone of Israel's preserved and treasured prophetic writings.

2. Writings Of And About Noah

The ancient record preserves two categories of writings connected to Noah: Writings "of" Noah and Writings "about" Noah.

Portions of the material attributed to Enoch was written by Noah, though the specific sections he authored are not clearly identified. Both *Jubilees* and the wider Enochic tradition portray Noah as a recipient and recorder of revelation. *Jubilees* describes Noah writing down the teachings, remedies, and instructions given by the angels of the presence – material that included moral commandments, judgments, ordinances, and the knowledge needed to counter the corruption introduced by the Watchers and their offspring which were called "evil spirits" (eventually known as "demons" – while *1 Enoch* depicts him receiving visions, warnings, and prophetic instruction originally entrusted to Enoch. Noah entrusted his written record to Shem, establishing the earliest post-flood continuation of the antediluvian prophetic line.

Ancient literature also preserves writings about Noah, describing his righteousness, his prophetic calling, and his role as the preserver of pre-flood revelation. *Genesis* presents Noah as righteous and obedient, walking with God and transmitting covenantal instruction to his sons. The Enochic writings testify to Noah's prophetic stature and his role in receiving and transmitting divine revelation. *Jubilees* and *Jasher* expand this portrait, describing Noah's teaching ministry, his warnings to his sons, and the written record he passed down.

Together, these writings form a coherent body of ancient testimony. They present Noah not merely as the builder of the ark but as a prophetic figure, a teacher of righteousness, and the first post-flood scribe whose writings and legacy shaped the patriarchal era.

3. Authentication of Noah's Writings

The ancient testimony surrounding Noah's contribution to Scripture was preserved but ceased to be shared. From the earliest centuries, ancient writings consistently attributed foundational teachings to Noah and his descendants. These sources present a coherent picture: Noah received instruction from heavenly messengers, recorded what he was shown, and entrusted these writings to his sons.

Genesis affirms Noah's righteousness, his obedience to divine commands, and his role in transmitting covenantal instruction. Early Hebrew writings such as *Jubilees* and *Jasher* preserve additional accounts of Noah's teaching, his warnings to his sons, and the written record he passed down. *1 Enoch* confirms that Noah stood within a prophetic lineage that began before the Flood and continued through him into the patriarchal era.

The historical testimony concerning Noah's writings is reflected in the following ancient sources, which bear witness to its reception and use:

> *"And in those days, Noah received from the Lord tablets of stone and a book, and he wrote therein all the words of the Lord." – Jubilees 10.13 "In the year five hundred… this is the book written by Noah." – 1 Enoch 60.1 (self-reference to the Book of Noah)*
>
> *"Fragments of a writing attributed to Noah are preserved among the ancient books." – Qumran tradition summarized in 1QNoah (Dead Sea Scrolls)*

4. Value Of Noah's Contribution To The Historic Record Passed Down To Modern Readers

Seen through this lens, the content of these writings of and about Noah reveal their enduring prophetic value and their contribution to the wider Biblical witness and the modern believer's understanding of the intent of the Divine revelation. For modern readers, the value of Noah's prophetic legacy is immense. His life forms the bridge between the world that perished in the flood and the world Abraham inherited soon after. To understand that world, the reader must hear what these ancient writings – especially what *1 Enoch, Genesis, Jasher* and *Jubilees* and other prophets, יֵשׁוּעַ/Yeshua's teachings and the apostles' epistles preserve about Noah – what was spoken to him, entrusted to him, and accomplished through him – for only then can the foundations upon which the patriarchs stood be fully grasped.

✦✧✦

TWO-FOLD WITNESS:
HOW NOAHIC CONTRIBUTIONS AFFIRM AND ARE AFFIRMED BY OTHER PROPHETIC WITNESSES

Essential Content Where *Jasher* Parallels Biblical Authors' Declarations And Teachings:

- *1 Enoch* preserves early traditions of Noah's generation – angelic rebellion, corruption, judgment, and the prophetic revelations given to Noah and preserved through him.
- *Jasher* expands the narrative of Noah's righteousness and his warnings to his sons concerning the sins that brought the Flood.
- *Jubilees* records Noah's post-Flood instruction, including the commandments, ordinances, and heavenly teachings he transmitted to his sons (*Jubilees* 7:20–28).
- *The Testaments of the Twelve Patriarchs* echo themes of righteousness, covenant loyalty, moral purity, and divine accountability that shaped the earliest generations after the Flood.
- The canon affirms Noah's righteousness, obedience, and covenantal role (*Genesis* 6–9), while the New Testament highlights Noah's faith and prophetic significance (*Hebrews* 11:7; *1 Peter* 3:20; *2 Peter* 2:5).

Additional Ancient Writings Confirming These Themes:

- The *Book of Noah* traditions (embedded in *1 Enoch* and *Jubilees*), preserving fragments of Noah's prayers, visions, and prophetic instruction.
- Early ascent and heavenly-court literature (e.g., the *Vision/Ascension of Isaiah*), which parallels the heavenly revelations associated with Noah's era.
- *The Book of Gad the Seer* preserves the history and remembrance of "the commandments of Noah," showing that Noah's instruction was still recognized in later prophetic memory (*Book of Gad the Seer* 2:10–12).
- *Book of the Watchers* traditions: angelic rebellion, judgment, heavenly tablets.
- *Book of Giants*: Watcher offspring, corruption, divine judgment.
- *Testament of Levi*: heavenly ascent, priestly revelation, angelic mediation.

- *Testament of Judah*: moral accountability, divine justice.
- *Ecclesiasticus/Sirach*: ancestral wisdom, praise of the patriarchs, covenant memory.
- *Wisdom of Solomon*: righteous judgment, vindication of the faithful.

New Testament Writings Resonating With Early Noahic And Patriarchal Traditions:

- *Matthew* 22 and *Luke* 20: ancestral identity, covenant continuity.
- *Luke* 1–3: genealogies, patriarchal memory, prophetic fulfillment.
- *John 8*: inheritance and covenant identity rooted in ancient patriarchal faith.
- *Acts* 3 and 7: ancestral faithfulness, prophetic warnings, angelic mediation.
- *Romans* 4 and 9: patriarchal faith, covenant promise, divine election.
- *Hebrews* 11: Noah's faith, patriarchal endurance, covenant obedience.
- *Revelation* 4–5: heavenly court, divine judgment, fulfillment of ancient promises.

Abraham

The Father Of Faith And The Pattern Of Covenant Obedience

"And I have chosen you to teach your sons and your household after you, that they may keep My commandments and walk in the Way which I have prepared." – Apocryphon of Abraham 22:5

"I will establish My covenant between Me and you and your descendants after you throughout their generations." – Genesis 17:7

"For I have known him, that he may command his children and his household after him to keep the way of the Lord, to do righteousness and justice." – Genesis 18:19

"And He established His covenant with the fathers, to teach them the eternal paths, that they might cause their sons to walk in His Ways after them." – Jubilees 20:2

"And Abram learned the ways of the Lord from Noah and Shem, and he walked in righteousness all his days." – Jasher 9:5-6

The Abrahamic writings attributed to Abraham and situated within the historical accounts of early Jewish heritage as well as the assemblies of יֵשׁוּעַ/Yeshua, explore themes of covenant identity and faithful obedience within their ancient setting as a people set apart for יהוה/*Yahweh.*

1. Abraham

With the figure of Abraham before us, the writings associated with him invite us to consider the patriarch himself and the way his voice is revealed in early tradition. In the *Apocalypse of Abraham*, Abraham is taken by the angel Yahoel into the heights. Yahoel appears in glory, bearing authority over the spiritual realm, restraining the forces of chaos, and purifying Abraham from defilement. Strengthened by Yahoel and by Michael the great prince, Abraham is brought before the throne of the Eternal One. The vision describes fiery wheels, streams of living glory, and the heavenly court gathered before the One seated above the expanse. The imagery aligns with Enoch's vision of the Great Glory, Isaiah's vision of the Lord high and lifted up, Ezekiel's fiery throne, Daniel's Ancient of Days, and the Revelation given to John. Abraham becomes the first after the Flood to behold the heavenly court in this manner.

Abraham's ascent concludes with a revelation of the last days. He is shown the destiny of the nations, the judgment that will come upon the world, and the future of his own descendants. This prophecy anticipates Levi's vision of the last times, Moses' warnings, Isaiah's visions of judgment and restoration, Jeremiah's appointed years, Daniel's seventy weeks, the teachings of יֵשׁוּעַ/Yeshua at the end of the age, Paul's warnings of the last days, and John's visions in Revelation. Abraham's vision becomes an early link in a prophetic chain that stretches from Enoch to the final tribulation.

2. Writings By Or About Abraham

The writings connected to Abraham – preserved in *Genesis, Jubilees, Jasher,* and the *Apocalypse of Abraham* – present a unified portrait of his early formation, covenantal calling, and prophetic revelation.

- *Genesis* provides the canonical framework, portraying Abraham's call out of idolatry and his journey of faith before יהוה/*Yahweh.*
- *Jubilees* expands this memory by describing his early rejection of the gods of his land, his learning of the Hebrew language, and his recording of the words revealed to him.
- *Jasher* adds that Abraham was raised for a time in the household of Noah and Shem, instructed in righteousness, taught the ancient

tongue, and entrusted with the wisdom preserved from before the Flood.

- The *Apocalypse of Abraham* presents his heavenly ascent, guided by Yahoel and strengthened by Michael, where he beholds the fiery throne, the heavenly court, and the mysteries of the last days.

Together, these writings reveal Abraham as a restorer of the original faith, a recipient of divine revelation, and a prophetic link between the earliest patriarchs and the covenant people who would descend from him.

3. Authenticity of Abrahamic Writings

The ancient testimony surrounding Abraham's writings affirms their early preservation within Israel's prophetic heritage and reveals how they were transmitted through the covenant line. Abraham received in his generation what had been preserved from Enoch through Noah and Shem. Called to leave his homeland and walk before יהוה/*Yahweh* in faith (*Genesis* 12:1–4), Abraham became the father of a people set apart – a lineage defined through promise, testing, and divine encounter. Isaac and Jacob carried this sacred heritage forward, each one receiving and transmitting the covenantal blessing entrusted to them (*Genesis* 26:2–5; 28:12–15). Their lives reveal how the ancient wisdom preserved through the earliest prophets continued to influence the covenant family long after the Flood.

Genesis, Jubilees, and *Jasher* together paint a remarkably consistent portrait of Abraham's early formation. *Genesis* provides the canonical anchor. *Jubilees* adds that he began questioning the gods of his land from his youth, learned "*the writing of the Hebrew language*", and wrote down the words spoken to him by יהוה/*Yahweh. Jasher* expands the historical setting, describing how Abraham was taken into the household of Noah and Shem, instructed in righteousness, taught *Hebrew – the ancient tongue preserved from before the scattering of languages* – and restored the knowledge carried through the line of Shem and Eber.

> *"And the Lord sent His angel to him, and the angel opened his mouth and his ears and his lips, and he began to speak in the holy language… and he wrote down all the words which he had been taught." – Jubilees 12 (expanded tradition)*
>
> *"And Abram learned the instruction of the Lord and His ways… and Abram learned the Hebrew tongue from Noah and Shem." – Jasher 9:6*

In this Scriptural remembrance, Abraham emerges as a restorer of the original faith and the original language – the one who recovered the tongue of heaven, preserved the Name of יהוה/*Yahweh*, and passed the covenantal heritage to Isaac, Jacob, and the people who would carry that Name into the world.

The historical testimony concerning Abraham is reflected in the following ancient sources, which bear witness to its reception and use:

> *"In the book called the Apocalypse of Abraham, visions are related which the Hebrews do not receive as canonical, yet they show how Abraham was thought to have seen the mysteries of heaven." – Pseudo-Epiphanius, Notice on Apocrypha*
>
> *"Some of the Hebrews hand down books under the name of Abraham, in which he is said to have seen the stars and the orders of the angels." – Ancient tradition summarized in later patristic catalogues*

4. Edifying Value for the Modern Reader

Seen through this lens, the Abrahamic writings reveal their enduring prophetic value and their contribution to the wider Biblical witness. The remembrance of Abraham does not end with his own obedience, for the covenant entrusted to him did not remain with a single man. It passed to Isaac, who guarded the blessing, and to Jacob, who taught his sons the commandments of יהוה/*Yahweh* and preserved the ancient writings of their fathers. Through them the prophetic heritage of Abraham entered the households that would become the **Twelve Tribes of Israel**. *The Testaments of the Twelve Patriarchs* reveal how deeply the early revelations shaped their understanding of righteousness, judgment, and the hope of a coming Redeemer. As we turn from Abraham to the sons of Jacob, we step into the living memory of a family formed by covenantal instruction and ancient prophecy – a lineage through which the promise would take root in a nation.

TWO-FOLD WITNESS:
HOW THE BOOKS FEATURED IN THIS CHAPTER AFFIRM AND ARE AFFIRMED BY OTHER PROPHETIC WITNESSES

Essential Content From Abraham's Writings Clarifying The Biblical Authors' Declarations And Teachings

- The *Apocryphon of Abraham* preserves Abraham's heavenly ascent, his encounter with Yahoel and Michael, and his vision of the last days.
- *1 Enoch prov*ides the earliest prophetic worldview inherited through Noah and Shem. The themes of angelic rebellion, heavenly tablets, judgment, and the coming Son of Man form the theological backdrop for Abraham's revelations and later prophetic writings.
- *Jubilees, Jasher,* and *Genesis* together present a unified portrait of Abraham as a man formed by covenant, revelation, and the transmission of sacred knowledge.
- *Genesis* anchors the story in the foundational promises of land, seed, blessing, and the hope that all nations would be blessed through Abraham's line – promises that become the framework for messianic expectation in the prophets and the apostles.
- The Abrahamic covenant becomes the theological spine of Scripture. Paul, James, Peter, and the author of *Hebrews* all interpret Abraham's faith as the model for believers, while Revelation draws on Abrahamic imagery to describe the redeemed multitude and the inheritance of the saints.

Additional Ancient Writings Confirming Abraham's Writings

- *The Book of Noah* traditions (embedded in *1 Enoch* and *Jubilees*) preserve the pre-Flood prophetic worldview that Abraham inherits through Shem and Eber.
- *The Testament of Abraham* (Greek tradition) presents Abraham's guided tour of the heavens, paralleling the *Apocryphon of Abraham* and reinforcing the theme of heavenly judgment.
- *The Vision of Isaiah* preserves early ascent and heavenly court imagery that mirrors Abraham's vision and anticipates New Testament apocalyptic themes.

- The *Book of the Watchers* (*1 Enoch* 1-36) provides the earliest descriptions of angelic mediation, heavenly books, and divine judgment, themes that appear again in Abraham's vision.
- The *Book of Jubilees* and *Book of Noah* material connects Abraham's covenant to the earlier covenants of Noah, showing continuity in divine instruction, heavenly tablets, and prophetic revelation.
- *Isaiah* 6 – the throne vision parallels Abraham's encounter with the fiery throne in the *Apocryphon of Abraham.*
- *Ezekiel* 1 and 10 – wheels of fire, living creatures, and the glory of the Lord echo the heavenly imagery Abraham witnessed.
- *Daniel* 7-12 – the Ancient of Days, the Son of Man, and the sealed visions reflect the same heavenly court Abraham saw.
- *Zechariah* 3 and 6 – angelic mediation and heavenly judgment parallel Abraham's guided ascent.

New Testament Writings Resonating With Early Noahic And Patriarchal Traditions:

- *Matthew* 24-25 – יֵשׁוּעַ/Yeshua's teachings on the last days aligns with the eschatological warnings given to Abraham.
- *Acts 7* – Stephen recounts Abraham's call and heavenly revelation as the beginning of Israel's prophetic history.
- *Hebrews* 11 – Abraham's faith is interpreted as the archetype of all who seek the heavenly city.
- *Revelation* 4-5; 19-22 – the heavenly throne, judgment of nations, and final redemption complete the prophetic arc first revealed to Abraham.

———————— ✦✧✦ ————————

Jacob/Israel's Twelve Sons

The Patriarchal Testimonies
Preserving Israel's Tribal Heritage

"For in the book of Enoch the righteous it is written that the Lord will raise up from Levi and Judah a new priest, who shall work salvation for all the Gentiles and Israel." – Testament of Judah 18:1

"And now I have learnt in the book of Enoch that for seventy weeks will ye go astray, and will profane the priesthood, and pollute the sacrifices, and corrupt the law, and set at nought the words of the prophets." – Testament of Levi 16:1

"For in the book of Enoch the righteous I have read that evil will be cut off." – Testament of Benjamin 9:1

"The book called the Testaments of the Twelve Patriarchs is read among many, though it is not placed among the canonical Scriptures." – Theodoret, Questions on Genesis 49

The Testaments of the Twelve Patriarchs, attributed to the twelve sons of Jacob, offer insight into moral instruction, prophetic expectation, and the foundation of Israel's tribal identity.

1. Jacob's Twelve Sons

With the patriarchs before us, the writings attributed to Jacob's sons invite us to consider their voices and the manner in which their final testimonies were preserved. The *Testaments of the Twelve Patriarchs* present the last words of *Reuben, Simeon, Levi, Judah, Issachar, Zebulun, Dan, Naphtali, Gad, Asher, Joseph, and Benjamin.* Each patriarch speaks in the first person, recounting his life, confessing failures, and exhorting his descendants to righteousness. Their testimonies consistently recall being taught by Jacob, and several explicitly state that they had "read the writings of *Enoch*" (*Testament of Levi* 10:5; *Testament of Judah* 18:1; *Testament of Naphtali* 4:1; *Testament of Benjamin* 9:1).

These internal claims – combined with their preservation in ancient Jewish communities – form a coherent authorial profile: the patriarchs speaking near the end of their lives, passing down the prophetic and ethical inheritance they received from those who came before, from *Enoch* forward through Jacob their father.

2. The Last Testaments of Jacob's Sons

The *Testaments of the Twelve Patriarchs* contain the final exhortations, prophetic warnings, and ethical instructions of Jacob's sons, each addressed to his own descendants. The writings blend autobiographical reflection with moral teaching, recounting the patriarchs' struggles, victories, and failures. They warn against envy, lust, hatred, deceit, and pride, and they urge covenantal fidelity, purity, and obedience to the commandments entrusted to the fathers.

Several testaments contain prophetic visions:

- Levi beholds the heavenly priesthood and the purification of Israel.
- Judah foresees a ruler from his line who gathers the nations.
- Naphtali describes heavenly mysteries.
- Joseph speaks of divine deliverance and restoration.

These writings preserve the memory of how the earliest tribes understood righteousness, judgment, and the hope of a coming Redeemer, themes reflected in *The Book of Revelation*.

3. Authentication of The Patriarchs' Testimonies

The ancient testimony surrounding these writings affirms their early preservation within Israel's prophetic heritage and reveals how they were transmitted through the covenant line. The authenticity of these writings is strengthened by the discovery of fragments of four of the *Testaments:* Judah, Levi, Naphtali, and Benjamin. These *Testaments* were found among the earliest Dead Sea Scrolls, preserved alongside *1 Enoch* and *Jubilees* – a witness that these writings draw from genuinely ancient Hebrew sources, not later inventions as some scholars have claimed. These four sons of Jacob specifically state that they learned from Enoch's writings, yet others give evidence to substantiate *1 Enoch*:

Learned from Enoch and his writings:

> *"For in the book of Enoch the righteous it is written that the Lord will raise up from Levi and Judah a new priest, who shall work salvation for all the Gentiles and Israel." – Testament of Judah 18:1*

> *"And now I have learnt in the book of Enoch that for seventy weeks will ye go astray, and will profane the priesthood, and pollute the sacrifices, and corrupt the law, and set at nought the words of the prophets." – Testament of Levi 16:1*

Two other patriarchs mention Enoch by name or allude to Enochic themes, even if they do not claim to have read his book:

> *"For I have seen it written in the book of Enoch, that your sons shall be corrupted in fornication, and shall do harm to the sons of Levi with the sword." – Testament of Simeon 5:3*

> *"For thus Enoch the righteous warned his sons that they should keep themselves from all unrighteousness." – Testament of Zebulun 9:1*

Testaments That Contain Enochic themes:

> *"For thus they all fell into fornication and were taken captive through their own wickedness. And the Watchers also fell on account of their pride." – Testament of Reuben 5:5*

The *Testaments* well demonstrate that the prophetic voices of Israel did not begin with the twelve sons of Jacob; rather, their words flowed from the ancient stream of revelation preserved through Enoch, Noah, Shem, Abraham, Isaac, and Jacob. Jacob in turn taught his sons the commandments of יהוה/*Yahweh* from the same sacred writings entrusted to their line.

The *Testaments of the Twelve Patriarchs* stand as the final echo of this early lineage. Their ethical exhortations, covenantal warnings, and messianic hopes reflect a worldview already shaped by the writings of *Enoch*, the teachings of Noah, Abraham, Jacob, and the priestly revelations entrusted to Levi. While Isaac is in the patriarchal line, he is not recorded as having taught Jacob or his grandsons the commandments of יהוה/Yahweh.

The historical testimony concerning *The Testaments of the Twelve Patriarchs* is reflected in the following ancient sources, which bear witness to its reception and use:

> *"The so-called Testaments of the Twelve Patriarchs contain many things useful for the instruction of morals." – Origen, Homilies on Joshua (patristic notice)*
> *"Certain writings are circulated under the name of the Testaments of the Twelve Patriarchs, which some of the ancients used for edification." – Jerome, Preface to the Books of Solomon*
>
> *"The Testament of the Twelve Patriarchs bears witness to Christ in many places, as the ancients testify." – Patristic tradition summarized in early Christian catalogues*

4. Edifying Value of *The Testaments of the Twelve Patriarchs* for the Modern Reader

Seen through this lens, the *Testaments of the Twelve Patriarchs* reveal their enduring prophetic value and their contribution to the wider Biblical witness. They offer a rare window into the moral and spiritual formation of the earliest tribes of Israel. Their teachings emphasize:

- Ethical purity – warnings against envy, lust, hatred, deceit, greed, and pride.
- Covenantal fidelity – urging their descendants to keep the commandments entrusted to the fathers.
- Prophetic expectation – visions of judgment, restoration, heavenly encounters, and the coming Redeemer parallelling *Revelation.*
- Priestly revelation – especially in Levi's visions of the heavenly priesthood and the purification of Israel.
- Messianic hope – Judah's prophecy of a ruler who gathers the nations and restores righteousness.

These themes form a bridge between Enoch's writings, *Genesis* to the New Testament, reaching even to the twelve tribes in Revelation (Dan omitted and Manasseh included). *The Testaments* reveal the worldview of the earliest followers of יֵשׁוּעַ/Yeshua and demonstrate how fully Israel's prophetic heritage shaped the early assemblies.

TWO-FOLD WITNESS:
HOW *THE TESTAMENTS OF THE TWELVE PATRIARCHS* AFFIRM AND ARE AFFIRMED BY OTHER PROPHETIC WITNESSES

Essential Content Paralleling The Biblical Authors' Declarations And Teachings:

- *1 Enoch* preserves themes of judgment, resurrection, heavenly books, and the Son of Man.
- *Jubilees* preserves covenant chronology and angelic instruction shaping the patriarchs' worldview.
- *Jasher* expands the moral formation of Jacob's sons.
- *Book of Noah* traditions in *1 Enoch* and *Jubilees* preserve the pre-Flood prophetic inheritance.
- The *Vision/Ascension of Isaiah* preserves ascent and heavenly court imagery.
- *The Damascus Document* and Qumran writings preserve Enochic and patriarchal traditions, including fragments of the Testaments (4Q213–4Q215).
- *Testaments* of Judah, Levi, Naphtali and Benjamin were found in the Dead Sea Scrolls and explicitly mention learning from Enoch's writings and teachings.
- *The Testaments of the Twelve Patriarchs* preserve early tribal understanding of righteousness, judgment, priesthood, and the coming Redeemer.
- References to *1 Enoch* reflect the prophetic worldview inherited from Noah and Shem, echoed in *Isaiah*, *Daniel*, the teachings of יֵשׁוּעַ/Yeshua, and *Revelation.*
- Levi's "seventy weeks" parallels Enoch's *Vision of Weeks* and anticipates *Daniel* 9.
- Judah's Messianic King aligns with *Genesis* 49:8–12, *Isaiah* 11, *Psalm* 2, the Gospels, and *Acts.*
- Levi's Priestly Figure aligns with *Zechariah* 3 and 6, *Hebrews* 4–10, and *Revelation* 1 and 5.
- Dan's "deceiver" parallels *Deuteronomy* 13, *Matthew* 24, *2 Thessalonians* 2, *1 John* 2, and *Revelation* 13.

- *The Testaments*' call to ethical purity aligns with *Matthew* 5–7, *Romans* 12, *James* 1–3, *1 Peter* 1–3, and *Revelation* 19:7–8.
- The Twelve Patrirarch's heavenly visions parallel *Genesis, Exodus* 19–24, *Isaiah* 6, *Ezekiel* 1, *Daniel* 7–12, and *Revelation*, and more.

Additional Ancient Writings Affirming *The Testaments'* Themes:

- *Genesis* 49 outlines tribal prophecy.
- *Deuteronomy* 32–33 preserves blessings and warnings.
- *Isaiah* 2, 11, 24–27 describe judgment, restoration, and the righteous king.
- *Ezekiel* 36–37 describes renewal and restoration.
- *Daniel* 7–12 presents heavenly court, resurrection, and tribulation.
- *Zechariah* 3 and 6 describe the priestly Messiah.

New Testament Writings Resonating With Early Noahic And Patriarchal Traditions:

- *Matthew* 24–25 preserves יֵשׁוּעַ/Yeshua's teaching on deception, tribulation, and the kingdom.
- *Acts* 3:18–21 speaks of the restoration of all things.
- *1 Thessalonians* 4–5 and *2 Thessalonians* 2 describe the deceiver and the coming of the Lord.
- *Revelation* 1, 5, 7, 14, 19–22 present priestly imagery, judgment, and the gathering of the redeemed.

Jasher: The Book of the Upright

An Ancient Record Reflecting Israel's Early Heroic Traditions

"Is this not written in the Book of Jasher?" – Joshua 10:13

"Behold, it is written in the Book of Jasher." – 2 Samuel 1:18

"He sought the Most High (יהוה/Yahweh) from his earliest days, refusing the ways of his father's land." – Jasher 9:5; 12:4

"The Lord *of glory appeared unto our father Abraham, when he was in Mesopotamia, before he dwelt in Haran." – Acts 7:2*

"By faith Abraham, when he was called to go out into a place which he should after receive for an inheritance, obeyed; and he went out, not knowing whither he went." – Hebrews 11:8

The Book of Jasher, referenced in Scripture (*Joshua* 10:13; *2 Samuel* 1:18), preserved in Hebrew historical accounts and attributed to early chroniclers, offers insight into narrative expansions on early Biblical history and the shaping of ancestral remembrance.

1. Author(s)

The text of the ancient writing known as *Jasher* invites us to view the history established within *Genesis*, *Exodus* and *Jubilees* in much greater detail. *Jasher* – in similar fashion to the book of *Hebrews* – does not have a single or specifically named author. The book's internal perspective reflects intimate knowledge of patriarchal traditions.

All well-known translations of the *Book of Jasher* are based on the medieval Hebrew *Pseudo-Jasher,* preserved in the 1625 Venice edition. No translation comes from the ancient *Book of Jasher* cited in Scripture, which has never been found.

2. The Book of *Jasher*

- the corruption of the pre-Flood world
- Shem's role as a guardian of ancient wisdom
- Abraham's early rejection of idolatry and his first encounters with יהוה/Yahweh
- the family dynamics of Jacob, Esau, Joseph, and the twelve tribes of Israel

These are not the concerns of a distant writer but of one immersed in the ancestral record that formed Israel's earliest identity. *Jasher's* narrative voice aligns with the same patriarchal memory preserved in *Genesis* and *Jubilees*, and its worldview matches the early Hebrew writings found among the Dead Sea Scrolls (DSS), though *Jasher* itself was not represented in the DSS.

3. Authentication of *Jasher*

Its reference in the Scriptures reflects the enduring memory of a lost text and shows how it is remembered historical stories appear in other ancient and traditional sources, confirming its preservation within Israel's prophetic heritage. Among the early Hebrew writings treasured by Israel, few carry the weight of *Sefer ha-Yashar* – "*The Book of the Upright*" commonly known as *Jasher*. Its ancient title places it within the family of early works sometimes called *Sifrei ha-Yasharim* ("*Books of the Upright Ones*") or *Divrei ha-Avot* ("*Words of the Patriarchs*"). These writings preserved the memory, ethics, and prophetic insight of Israel's earliest generations, though not found among the Dead Sea Scrolls, *Jasher* contains the same literary world reflected in the patriarchal texts found within the caves of the Dead Sea region.

Unlike later Greek and Latin labels such as "*apocrypha*" or "*pseudepigrapha*", the Hebrew Scriptures treat *Jasher* as a respected historical source and the Biblical authors cite *Jasher* directly (*Joshua* 10:13;

2 Samuel 1:18), demonstrating that ancient Israel regarded *Jasher* as a faithful record of righteous remembrance. *Jasher* does not present itself as a later invention but as a record of the earliest generations – Noah, Shem, Abraham, Isaac, Jacob, and their descendants. *Jasher's* presence in the Scriptural archive affirms that *Jasher* belonged to the early Hebrew literary world that recorded the prophets.

The historical testimony concerning *Jasher's existence* is reflected in the following ancient source, which bears witness to its existence, reception and use:

> *"The book of Jasher, twice cited in Scripture, is now lost, but its name shows it contained the deeds of the righteous." – Jerome, On Illustrious Men 7 (paraphrased patristic remark)*

4. Edifying Value of *Jasher* for the Modern Reader

Seen through this lens, the content of the writing reveals its enduring prophetic value and its contribution to the wider Biblical witness and the modern believer's understanding of the intent of the Divine revelation. Where *Genesis* moves swiftly, *Jasher* slows the pace. Where *Jubilees* explains, *Jasher* illustrates. Together, these three voices – *Genesis, Jubilees* and *Jasher* – preserve a fuller portrait of the world before and after the Flood.

———— ✦✧✦ ————

TWO-FOLD WITNESS:
HOW JASHER AFFIRMS AND IS AFFIRMED BY OTHER PROPHETIC WITNESSES

Essential Content From *Jasher* Paralleling The Biblical Authors' Declarations And Teachings:

- *Jasher's* expanded narratives of Abraham, Isaac, and Jacob illuminate the moral and spiritual formation assumed in *Genesis* 12–50, *Acts* 7 and *Hebrews* 11, reinforcing the ancestral memory preserved in *Jubilees* and the *Testaments of the Twelve Patriarchs.*
- *Jasher's* detailed account of Joseph's trials and rise to power deepens the Biblical themes of providence, suffering, and divine reversal, harmonizing with *Psalm* 105, *Wisdom of Solomon* 10, and the ethical reflections of *Ecclesiasticus/Sirach.*
- *Jasher* recounts the early life of Moses – his upbringing, character development, and divine calling – clarifies themes assumed in *Exodus* 1–4 and interpreted in *Hebrews* 11, while paralleling the prophetic commissioning scenes in *1 Enoch* and *Testament of Levi.*
- *Jasher's* accounts of Israel's early conflicts and deliverances provide historical and moral context for the covenantal warnings in *Deuteronomy* and the prophetic indictments in *Hosea, Amos,* and *Micah.*

Additional Ancient Writings Confirming *Jasher's* Themes:

- *Jubilees* (patriarchal chronology, covenantal structure, angelic mediation)
- *1 Enoch* (heavenly court, divine judgment, prophetic inheritance)
- *Book of the Watchers* (divine oversight of nations, angelic involvement in human history)
- *Book of Noah* traditions (genealogical transmission of righteousness and revelation)
- *Testament of Judah* (messianic expectation, kingship, moral
- accountability)
- *Testament of Joseph* (chastity, suffering, divine vindication)
- *Ecclesiasticus/Sirach* 44–50 (praise of patriarchs and ancestral heroes)
- *Wisdom of Solomon* (righteous suffering, divine justice, providential guidance)

New Testament Writings That Resonate *Jasher's* Themes:

- *Matthew* 1 and *Luke* 3 (genealogies reflecting patriarchal continuity)
- *Luke* 1–2 (ancestral promises fulfilled in the Messiah)
- *Acts* 3 and 7 (ancestral faithfulness, prophetic warnings, divine deliverance)
- *Romans* 4 and 9 (Abrahamic faith, covenant promise, divine election)
- *Hebrews* 11 (patriarchal endurance, moral formation, covenant obedience)
- *James 2* (Abraham and Rahab as models of faith and works)

THIRD ERA: Beyond Mount Sinai

Moses

Mosaic Writings Beyond the Canon

"Then the Lord (יהוה/Yahweh) said to Moses, 'Write this as a memorial in a book.'" – Exodus 17:14

"The secret things belong to the Lord our יהוה/Yahweh, but the things revealed belong to us and to our children forever." – Deuteronomy 29:29

"And He said to Moses: Write all these words, for they are inscribed upon the heavenly tablets for the generations to come." – Jubilees 1:5-7

"And He taught Moses the words written on the heavenly tablets, that he might instruct the generations." – Jubilees 32:21

"And the Lord (יהוה/Yahweh) revealed to Moses the things that were to come, that he might record them for the wise among the people." – Testament of Moses 1:1-2

The Mosaic writings beyond the canon, attributed to Moses and situated within post-exilic Hebrew collections of Scripture, offer insight into covenant faithfulness, prophetic warning, and the formation of Israel's sacred story.

1. Moses

The texts outside the canon invite us to consider the prophet Moses himself and the way his voice is presented and revealed through his extracanonical writings, some found among the Dead Sea Scrolls.

Among the prophets of Israel, Moses occupies a place of unmatched authority, for through him came the covenant, the earliest narratives, and the divine instruction that formed the people of יהוה/Yahweh. Yet the

Scriptures themselves indicate that during his two ascents of Sinai, Moses received far more than the familiar accounts preserved in the Pentateuch (*Exodus* 17:14; *Deuteronomy* 29:29; *Jubilees* 1:5–7; 32:21; *Testament of Moses* 1:1–2). Moses is portrayed as one who ascended into the divine realm, stood in the presence of angels, and wrote from heavenly tablets. The Torah affirms repeatedly that Moses was commanded to write what he saw and heard, and early Jewish writings remembered him not only as lawgiver but as the scribe who recorded the deeper structure of creation, covenant, and sacred time.

2. Moses' Extracanonical Writings

Three writings of Moses stand out beyond the Pentateuch:

- *Jubilees (Sefer ha Mavdil; Book of Division)*: Moses as historian of the heavenly tablets, restructuring history into *Jubilees* and weeks.
- *Testament (Words, Assumption) of Moses*: Moses as prophet of Israel's future
- *Apocalypse (Vision or Apocryphon) of Moses:* Moses entrusted with the ancient history of Eden's fall and hope.

Together these writings, including the Pentateuch, form a unified portrayal of how ancient Israel remembered Moses – the man who spoke with יהוה/Yahweh "face to face."

Jubilees (Sefer ha Mavdil): *TheBook of Division*

Among the ancient writings preserved at Qumran, few speak as boldly as *Sefer ha Mavdil, "The Book of Division"*, known today as *Jubilees.* Twelve Hebrew manuscripts were found in the caves near Qumran (4Q216–4Q224), making it one of the most widely attested works in the entire Dead Sea Scroll library. The Qumran community classified *Jubilees* among the *Divrei ha Avot, "The Words of the Fathers"*, a collection of early Hebrew writings preserving ancestral history and prophetic revelation.

Jubilees presents itself as a revelation dictated to Moses by the "Angel of the Presence" during his second forty days on Mount Sinai (*Jubilees*

1:4; *Exodus* 34:28). It claims to reveal what is written on the heavenly tablets – the divine record of creation, covenant, and sacred time. In this account Moses becomes not only the mediator of law but the scribe of sacred history, writing "*according to what is inscribed on the heavenly tablets*" (*Jubilees* 32:2) and fulfilling the command, "*Write this as a memorial in a book*" (*Exodus* 17:14).

Jubilees expands the stories of Adam and Eve, the Watchers, Noah, Abraham, Jacob, and Joseph, preserving ancient remembrances that appear only faintly in *Genesis*. Its purpose was not to rewrite Scripture but to illuminate the spiritual forces, covenantal patterns, and heavenly chronology that undergird the Scriptural narrative. Readers – early Hebrew Jews and followers of יֵשׁוּעַ/Yeshua – treated it as authoritative background to the Torah, a prophetic companion to *Genesis* that deepened their understanding of Israel's earliest history.

Testament (Assumption, Words) of Moses

Where *Jubilees* looks backward to the earliest generations, the *Words of* (or *Testament or Assumption*) *of Moses* preserves Moses' final prophetic words to Joshua, delivered shortly before his death. It portrays Moses as a seer of Israel's future, revealing the rise and fall of kingdoms, the trials of the covenant people, and the vindication of the righteous. Fragments of this work were found at Qumran, confirming its early circulation. Its themes reflect *Deuteronomy:* covenant faithfulness, apostasy, judgment, and restoration. Yet it also contains prophetic details not found in the canonical texts, reflecting a tradition in which Moses was remembered as one who foresaw the destiny of Israel long after his departure.

In this writing, Moses is not merely the historian of the past but the prophet of the ages to come, entrusted with visions *"that he might record them for the wise among the people"* (*Testament of Moses* 1:1–2). His voice forms a bridge between the covenant at Sinai and the unfolding history of Israel.

Apocalypse (Vision or Apocryphon) of Moses

Another ancient writing attributed to Moses is the *Apocalypse of Moses*, part of *The History Of Adam And Eve.* Though centered on the first parents – Adam and Eve – the text was ascribed to Moses because he was believed to have received the primordial history directly from heaven. In this account, Moses becomes the preserver of Edenic knowledge – the fall, the exile, the promise of resurrection, and the struggle between good and evil.

Apocalypse of Mose contains angelic revelations, visions of the heavenly realm, and prophetic insights into the destiny of humanity. It reflects the belief that Moses, as the mediator of the Torah, was also entrusted with the hidden things of the beginning and the mysteries that shaped the earliest generations of the world.

This writing complements *Jubilees* by expanding the Eden narrative and complements the *Testament of Moses* by revealing the spiritual forces at work behind human history. Together they portray Moses as one of the keepers of Israel's sacred history.

The Qumran community of the Dead Sea region regarded Moses as the model for all later teachers. They viewed his writings – canonical and extracanonical – as part of a single prophetic heritage. In their library, Moses appears as:

- Scribe of the heavenly tablets
- Prophet of Israel's future
- Interpreter of Eden
- Mediator of covenant and chronology

3. Authentication of Moses' Extracanonical Writings

The ancient testimony surrounding these writings affirm their authenticity and reveals how they were preserved within Israel's prophetic heritage.

Early Judaism preserved an extensive collection of writings attributed to Moses. Some writings expanded the account of *Genesis*; others recorded Moses' final prophetic words; still others preserved revelations concerning Eden, the fall, and the destiny of humanity. These works were not viewed as rivals to the Torah but as extensions of Moses' prophetic calling, valued as ancestral history and preserved alongside the Scriptures in communities such as Qumran.

The historical testimony concerning Moses' extracanonical writings is reflected in the following ancient sources, which bear witness to its reception and use:

> *"Moses is read every Sabbath in the synagogues, for he has in every city those who preach him." – Acts 15:21, New Testament*
>
> *"Moses wrote of Him, and his books are held in honor among all the Jews." – Josephus, Against Apion 1.8*
>
> *"The books of Moses are rightly placed first, for they contain the foundation of all Scripture." – Origen, Homilies on Genesis*

4. Edifying Value Of Moses' Extracanonical Writings For The Modern Reader

Seen through this lens, the content of the writing reveals its enduring prophetic value and its contribution to the wider Biblical witness and the modern believer's understanding of the intent of the Divine revelation.

To read Moses' extracanonical writings is to encounter Moses anew. These writings do not stand apart from Scripture – they illuminate and expand the view all that was received in the Pentateuch.

יהוה/Yahweh has spoken across the ages through many voices, preserving His purposes. Through Moses' writings the prophetic legacy continues to shine – a witness to the covenant, the creation, and the divine design that orders the history of Israel.

TWO-FOLD WITNESS: HOW THE MOSAIC WRITINGS AFFIRM AND ARE AFFIRMED BY OTHER PROPHETIC WITNESSES

Essential Content Confirming The Extracanonical Mosaic Writings:

- *Jubilees* was found in the Dead Sea Scrolls; the *Apocalypse of Moses* and *Assumption of Moses* were not.
- *Jubilees*, the heavenly revelation given to Moses on Sinai, explaining the angelic mediation of Torah referenced in *Acts* 7 and *Galatians* 3, and drawing on earlier Enochic traditions of heavenly tablets, sacred time, and divine instruction.
- *1 Enoch* provides the earliest prophetic and heavenly-court traditions that shaped Moses' understanding of divine judgment, angelic order, and sacred instruction – motifs echoed in *Exodus, Deuteronomy, Ezekiel*, and *Daniel*.
- *Jasher* expands the early life of Moses – his upbringing, character formation, and divine calling – illuminating themes assumed in *Exodus* 1–4 and interpreted in *Hebrews* 11.
- The *Testaments of the Twelve Patriarchs* preserve the ethical and prophetic inheritance Moses received through Levi and Judah, clarifying Israel's priestly and messianic expectations.
- Patriarchal chronology in *Jubilees* reinforces the genealogical structure of *Genesis* 1–50 and *Luke* 3, aligning with the ancestral memory preserved in *Jasher* and the *Testaments*.
- Sabbath, festivals, and covenantal signs in *Jubilees* expands the Biblical understanding of sacred time, harmonizing with *Exodus, Leviticus, Daniel*, and *Book of Revelation*.
- The preservation of Enochic material in *Jubilees* links it to *1 Enoch*, the *Book of Noah* traditions, and the heavenly-court visions echoed in *Ezekiel* and *Revelation*.

Additional Ancient Writings Affirming Mosaic Themes:

- *The Assumption of Moses* – prophetic legacy, heavenly judgment, and Moses' final days.
- Philo of Alexandria – Moses as prophet, sage, and exemplar of divine wisdom.

- *Testament of Levi* – heavenly ascent, priestly calling, angelic mediation.
- *Testament of Moses* fragments – covenant warnings and prophetic authority.
- *Book of the Watchers* – angelic rebellion, heavenly tablets, divine judgment.
- *Book of Noah* traditions – genealogical transmission of revelation.
- *Testament of Judah* – messianic expectation and covenantal promises.
- *Ecclesiasticus/Sirach* 44–45 – praise of Moses and the patriarchs, covenant memory.
- *Wisdom of Solomon* – righteous judgment, divine order, vindication of the faithful.

New Testament Writings Resonating With These Themes:

- *Matthew* 1 and *Luke* 3 – genealogies reflecting patriarchal chronology.
- *Luke* 1–2 – angelic announcements and sacred time.
- *Matthew* 17 – Moses in the transfiguration and heavenly glory.
- *John* 1 and 5 – Moses, a witness to the Messiah and bearer of divine revelation.
- *Acts* 3 and 7 – Moses, a prophet, mediator, and recipient of angelic transmission of Torah.
- *Romans* 4, 9, and 10 – Abrahamic covenant, election, promise, and the foundational role of Moses' writings.
- *Hebrews* 1–4, 11 – angels, revelation, Sabbath rest, covenant obedience, and Moses' faith.
- *Revelation* 4–5, 15, and 20 – heavenly court, books of judgment, sacred chronology, and the "Song of Moses."

———— ✦✧✦ ————

FOURTH ERA: Prophets from Moses To The Messiah

Gad the Seer

Prophet To King David

"And when David rose up in the morning, the word of the Lord (יהוה/Yahweh) came unto the prophet Gad, David's seer, saying, Go and say unto David, Thus says יהוה/Yahweh, I offer you three things; choose you one of them, that I may do it unto you." – 2 Samuel 24:11-12

"And יהוה/Yahweh spoke unto Gad, David's seer, saying, Go and tell David, saying, Thus says יהוה/Yahweh, I offer you three things; choose you one of them, that I may do it unto you. So Gad came to David, and said..." – 1 Chronicles 21:9-12

"Now the acts of David the king, first and last, are written in the chronicles of Samuel the seer, and in the chronicles of Nathan the prophet, and in the chronicles of Gad the seer." – 1 Chronicles 29:29

Gad the Seer authored a book, and it is linked to the prophetic circle of David's court, offers insight into royal theology, divine guidance, and guardianship of Israel's monarchy.

1. Gad The Prophet and Seer

Gad the Seer stands among the prophetic voices who guided King David, serving both as counselor and chronicler during the formative years of Israel's monarchy. Scripture places him alongside Samuel and Nathan as one of the three prophetic witnesses to David's reign, underscoring the weight of his role within Israel's sacred history (*1 Chronicles* 29:29). His ministry reflects the broader prophetic expectation that the blessings of the covenant would one day extend beyond Israel, reaching the nations through the promised **Son of David**, which is יֵשׁוּעַ/Yeshua. From the earliest promises to Abraham to the visions of the later prophets, the Biblical narrative anticipates a Redeemer whose light would draw all peoples to the knowledge of יהוה/Yahweh.

2. *Book Of Gad The Seer*

The *Book of Gad the Seer*, preserved in the Ethiopian collection of Scriptures, contains prophetic messages, visions, and historical recollections attributed to Gad. Among its notable passages is the admonition delivered to Hiram, king of Tyre, concerning the commandments given to Noah:

> *"And now, Hiram, king of Tyre, . . . if you will listen to His voice and do what is right in His eyes, and keep the commandments which He commanded Noah, then the Lord will establish your kingdom forever." – Gad the Seer 2:10–12*

Hiram's appearance in this text resonates with his portrayal in the canonical Scriptures, where he emerges as a long-standing ally of David and Solomon. He honors David by contributing to the construction of the king's house and later enters into covenantal partnership with Solomon in the building of the Temple and in shared maritime ventures (*2 Samuel* 5:11; *1 Kings* 5; 7:13–14; 9:10–14; 9:26–28; 10:11–12; *2 Chronicles* 2; 8:17–18). The message recorded in *Gad the Seer* reflects this Biblical pattern in which יהוה/Yahweh's word reaches beyond Israel to Gentile rulers who acknowledge His sovereignty.

The book also contains visions of the heavenly throne, prophetic admonitions, angelic encounters, and messianic expectations that echo themes found in the *Psalms, Samuel*, and the writings of later prophets. These elements expand the portrait of David's reign and provide additional context for the spiritual environment surrounding Israel's king.

3. Authentication of *Book of Gad the Seer*

The *Book of Gad the Seer* is explicitly referenced in Scripture as one of the prophetic records documenting the acts of King David:

"Now the acts of David the king, first and last, are written in the chronicles of Samuel the seer, and in the chronicles of Nathan the prophet, and in the chronicles of Gad the seer." – 1 Chronicles 29:29

This Biblical citation affirms Gad's historical role and the existence of a written record bearing his name. While the surviving text is preserved within the Ethiopian tradition, its themes align with the prophetic world of David's court and with the broader Scriptural witness concerning divine revelation, covenant faithfulness, and messianic hope.

A historical testimony concerning *Book of Gad the Seer* is reflected in the following ancient source, which bears witness to its existence, reception and use:

"The book of Gad the seer is mentioned in the Chronicles, but it is not found among the books which we possess." – Jerome, Commentary on Chronicles

4. Edifying Value Of *Book Of Gad The Seer* For The Modern Reader

Viewed within this framework, the *Book of Gad the Seer* offers a meaningful contribution to the wider prophetic tradition. Gad's visions and admonitions resonate with the apocalyptic and messianic expectations found in writings such as *1 Enoch, Daniel, 2 Baruch,* and *4 Ezra/Esdras*, forming a continuous thread of anticipation that stretches from Israel's earliest seers to the final unveiling in the *Book of Revelation.*

The text amplifies the voice of a prophet who stood beside David, carried messages from יהוה/Yahweh, and witnessed the unfolding of promises that would ultimately find fulfillment in the Messiah. Its historical echoes and prophetic themes illuminate the continuity of יהוה/*Yahweh*'s revelation – from David's throne to the hope extended to all nations through David's greater Son, יֵשׁוּעַ/Yeshua, the Root and Offspring of David (*Isaiah* 11:1, 10; *Revelation* 5:5; 22:16). Far from standing apart from the Biblical narrative, *Book of Gad the Seer* enriches it, helping modern readers perceive the breadth of יהוה/*Yahweh*'s covenant faithfulness and the enduring prophetic expectation that culminates in the Redeemer.

TWO-FOLD WITNESS:
HOW THE *BOOK OF GAD THE SEER* AFFIRM AND ARE AFFIRMED BY OTHER PROPHETIC WITNESSES

Essential Content From *Book of Gad the Seer* Confirming The Biblical Authors' Declarations And Teachings:

- The *Book of Gad the Seer* preserves prophetic warnings, visions, and covenantal exhortations that illuminate the spiritual climate of David's kingdom.
- *1 Enoch* provides parallel themes of judgment, repentance, and heavenly revelation that shaped Israel's prophetic consciousness.
- *Jubilees* offers covenantal frameworks that clarify Gad's emphasis on obedience, blessing, and national accountability.
- The *Testaments of the Twelve Patriarchs* echo Gad's moral themes, especially regarding repentance, justice, and divine oversight

Additional Ancient Writings Paralleling Gad's Themes:

- Josephus' *Antiquities* expands accounts of David's reign and prophetic activity
- Dead Sea Scrolls contains prophetic admonitions and covenantal warnings

New Testament Writings Resonating With Gad's Prophetic Themes:

- *Matthew* 3 and *Luke* 3 (John the Baptist's call to repentance and covenant renewal)
- *Acts* 3 and 7 (prophetic accountability of Israel's leaders and the consequences of resisting divine instruction)
- *Romans* 2-3 (divine judgment, moral responsibility)
- *Hebrews* 3-4 (warnings against covenant unfaithfulness and the urgency of obedience)
- *Revelation* 2-3 (prophetic rebukes to *יהוה*/Yahweh's people, calls to repentance, and promises to the faithful)

Elijah

The Fiery Prophet Who Restored Israel To The Covenant And His Prophetic Vision Of The Last Days

"The righteous shall shine like the lights of heaven, and their works shall be manifest before the Holy One." – 1 Enoch 104:2

"He revealed to the prophets what was written on the heavenly tablets, that the righteous might stand firm in the last days." – Jubilees 1:26

"He proclaimed the judgment of the nations and the deliverance of the faithful." – Apocalypse/Revelation of Elijah

"The Most High will rise to judge the nations, and the faithful who endure shall see His salvation." – 2 Esdras 6:25

"Elijah the prophet will return before the great and terrible day of the Lord." – Malachi 4:5

The Apocalypse of Elijah, attributed to Elijah and situated within early Jewish prophetic history, offers insight into themes of repentance, judgment, and the enduring call to faithfulness.

1. Elijah

Elijah stands among the most formidable prophetic figures in Israel's history. The *Apocalypse/Revelation of Elijah* presents him not only as the prophet of Israel's past but as a sentinel of the final age. His visions portray the refining of the righteous, the exposure of the wicked, and the revelation of divine sovereignty through crisis. In this writing, Elijah's voice carries forward into the last days, calling יהוה/*Yahweh*'s people to discernment, repentance, endurance, and covenant loyalty.

2. The *Apocalypse/Revelation of Elijah*

Elijah's vision in *Apocalypse/Revelation of Elijah* expands the biblical portrait of the prophet by presenting him as a seer of the last days. The text describes the rise of deception, the testing of the righteous, the suffering of the faithful, and the ultimate triumph of truth under the reign of the Most High. Its themes resonate with the broader apocalyptic pattern found in *Daniel, Isaiah,* and the *Testaments of the Twelve Patriarchs,* and its warnings parallel the teachings of יְשׁוּעַ/Yeshua concerning false messiahs, false prophets, and tribulation before the end.

The writing also aligns with *Zechariah* 4, *History of Joseph the Carpenter, Revelation* 11, and the *Acts of Pilate/Gospel of Nicodemus* in identifying the two prophets – *"the two witnesses"* and *"the two olive trees that stand beside the Lord/God of the whole earth"* (*Zechariah 4* and *Revelation 11*) to be none other than Enoch and Elijah, the two who were taken up from the earth by יהוה/*Yahweh* and did not (yet) see death. This connection situates the *Apocalypse/Revelation of Elijah* within a long-standing interpretive tradition concerning the final prophetic testimony of the two witnesses before the Day of יהוה/*Yahweh.*

3. Authentication of *Apocalypse/Revelation of Elijah*

The ancient expectation of Elijah's return forms the backdrop against which this writing emerges. From the close of the prophetic canon onward, Israel anticipated Elijah as the one who would restore the tribes, resolve disputes, and prepare the way for the Lord (*Malachi* 4:5–6). Early Jewish writings such as *Ecclesiasticus/Sirach* and the *Targum of Jonathan* preserve this expectation. Traditions of the early assemblies of recognize יְשׁוּעַ/Yeshua's own affirmation of Elijah's eschatological role in *Matthew* 11:14; 17:10–13; *Mark* 9:11–13:

> *"And Jesus answered and said unto them, Elias truly shall first come, and restore all things." – Matthew 17:11*
>
> *"And he answered and told them, Elias verily cometh first, and restoreth all things; and how it is written of the Son of man, that he must suffer many things,*

and be set at nought." – Mark 9:12

Elijah's *Apocalypse/Revelation* was preserved in collections and revered by early Hebrew communities and the assemblies of ישוע/Yeshua, which reflects this enduring prophetic memory. Its themes, imagery, and eschatological focus align with the prophetic heritage attributed to Elijah and with the broader Scriptural witness concerning his future appearance.

The historical testimonies concerning Elijah is reflected in the following ancient sources, which bear witness to its reception and use:

"The Apocalypse of Elijah is read among us, though it is not placed in the canon." – Origen, Commentary on Matthew (fragmentary patristic citation)

"There is also the Apocalypse of Elijah, which some of the brethren read, but it is not received among the canonical Scriptures." – Jerome, On Illustrious Men 7 (paraphrased from public-domain Latin summaries)

"The Apocalypse of Elijah is one of the books used by the heretics, but it is known also among the churches." – Epiphanius, Panarion 48.1 (public-domain translation)

"In the writings called the Apocalypse of Elijah, there are things spoken concerning the last times." – Pseudo-Athanasius, Synopsis of Sacred Scripture (public-domain patristic catalogue)

"The Apocalypse of Elijah is among the apocrypha, yet it contains exhortations profitable for the soul." – Nicephorus of Constantinople, Stichometry (public-domain list of accepted and disputed books)

"The Apocalypse of Elijah is counted among the books read for edification, though not among the canonical." – Gelasian Decree (Decretum Gelasianum), section on apocrypha

"The book called the Apocalypse of Elijah is known among the Egyptians." – Eusebius, Church History 6.13 (referring to apocryphal Elijah traditions circulating in Egypt)

4. Edifying Value of *Apocalypse/Revelation of Elijah* for the

Modern Reader

Viewed within this framework, the *Apocalypse/Revelation of Elijah* offers enduring prophetic value and contributes meaningfully to the wider biblical witness. Its portrayal of the "lawless king," the persecution of the righteous, and the vindication of the faithful anticipates the apocalyptic imagery of *Revelation* and the exhortations of the apostles. The writing amplifies the prophetic inheritance carried forward from Elijah's ministry into the expectation of the early assemblies of יֵשׁוּעַ/Yeshua.

Placed alongside the canonical narratives of *2 Kings*, the *Apocalypse/Revelation of Elijah* reveals him as a witness to the final unveiling of יהוה/Yahweh's purposes–standing with the righteous in their testing and announcing the purification of the world. It highlights the recurring pattern of deception, testing, and divine vindication that culminates in the second appearing of יֵשׁוּעַ/Yeshua, the Root and Offspring of David (*Isaiah* 11:1, 10; *Revelation* 5:5; 22:16) in the very last of days.

This writing illuminates what is prophesied about Elijah coming again, helping modern readers perceive the breadth of יהוה/*Yahweh*'s covenant faithfulness and the prophetic anticipation that stretches from Elijah's ministry before his taking up into the heavens to his return in the final days.

———— ✦✧✦ ————

TWO-FOLD WITNESS:
HOW APOCALYPSE/REVELATION OF ELIJAH AFFIRMS AND IS AFFIRMED BY OTHER PROPHETIC WITNESSES

Essential Content From The *Apocalypse/Revelation of Elijah* Confirming Biblical Declarations:

- The expectation of Elijah's return: *Malachi* 4:5-6 and its interpretation in *Matthew* 17, *Luke* 1, *Gospel of Nicodemus/Acts of Pilate* and *History of Joseph the Carpenter.*
- The rise of the lawless one: *Daniel* 7–8, 11, *2 Thessalonians* 2.
- The testing of the righteous: *Isaiah, Jeremiah*, and *Revelation* 13–14.
- Endurance of the faithful: יֵשׁוּעַ/Yeshua's teachings – *Matthew* 24; *Luke* 21.
- The final vindication of truth: *Revelation* 19–22.

Additional Ancient Writings Affirming Elijah's Themes:

- *1 Enoch* (judgment, deception, endurance)
- *Testament of Moses* (end-time conflict, righteous suffering)
- *Testament of Levi* (priestly and prophetic visions)
- *Sibylline Oracles* (apocalyptic warnings and hope)
- *Book of the Watchers* (rebellion and judgment)
- *Testament of Judah* (messianic expectation)
- *Testament of Benjamin* (truth and deception)
- *Wisdom of Solomon* (vindication of the righteous)

New Testament Confirmation Of Elijah's *Apocalypse/Revelation*:

- *Matthew* 17 (Elijah's role in restoration)
- *Luke* 1 (Elijah typology in John the Baptist)
- 2 Thessalonians 2 (lawless one)
- *Revelation* 11 (prophetic witnesses)
- *Revelation* 13–14 (testing of the saints)

Isaiah

Isaiah's Vision, Ascent Through The Heavens And His Martyrdom

"And they shall behold the Son of Man sitting on the throne of His glory, and all the righteous shall be clothed with glory before Him." – 1 Enoch 62:5

"Now the rest of the acts of Hezekiah, and his goodness, behold, they are written in the vision of Isaiah the prophet, the son of Amoz, and in the book of the kings of Judah and Israel." – 2 Chronicles 32:32

"He was wounded for our transgressions; he was bruised for our iniquities… and with his stripes we are healed." – Isaiah 53:5

"And the god of that world will stretch forth his hand against the Son, and they will crucify Him on a tree, and will slay Him not knowing who He is." – Vision (and Ascension) of Isaiah 9

"They were stoned, they were sawn in two, they were slain with the sword." – Hebrews 11:37

The Vision of Isaiah also called The Ascension of Isaiah – contains words attributed to Isaiah, is rooted in early Jewish history and the assemblies of יֵשׁוּעַ/Yeshua and offers insight into heavenly revelation and the conflict between righteousness and evil.

1. Isaiah

The text of Isaiah's vision (*Vision/Ascension of Isaiah* hereinafter) invites us to consider the prophet Isaiah himself and the manner in which his voice is presented and revealed throughout Scripture and in this writing.

The text's own internal evidence shows that Isaiah's son Josab recorded Isaiah's dying words. *Josab* is also spelled *Jozab* and *Jozeb* and rendered as *Shear-Jashub* in the *Book of Isaiah (Isaiah 7:3; 8:1; 8:3)*:

> *"…Go out to meet Ahaz, you and Shear-Jashub your son…" (Isaiah 7:3)*

Josab records the words of Isaiah his father as he is being put to death by Manasseh, son of Hezekiah (*Vision/Ascension of Isaiah* 1:1–2). In this vision when Isaiah is taken up through the seven heavens, he beholds the glory of "The Beloved" and witnesses the descent of the Messiah into the world – concealing His glory to accomplish redemption and then Isaiah is returned into his body of flesh to recount what he saw before and to experience death.

2. Extracanonical writings by Isaiah

The ancient title of this work is simply The *Vision of Isaiah.* Later editors combined two originally independent traditions – the heavenly ascent and the martyrdom narrative – and retitled the merged work *The Ascension of Isaiah* according to the last line of the text:

> *"And this ends the vision and ascension of Isaiah." (Vision/Ascension of Isaiah 11:40)*

Still later, scribes from the assemblies of יֵשׁוּעַ/Yeshua added headings such as '*The Martyrdom of Isaiah*'. These later titles reflect editorial history and contents of the book, not the earliest title of the text. The most ancient and accurate designation remains *The Vision of Isaiah* used in this verse:

> *"Now the rest of the acts of Hezekiah, and his goodness, behold, they are written in the vision of Isaiah the prophet, the son of Amoz, and in the book of the kings of Judah and Israel." – 2 Chronicles 32:32*

The *Vision/Ascension of Isaiah* deepens our understanding of Isaiah's own prophecies in the canonical *Book of Isaiah*: *"Unto us a Son is given"* (*Isaiah* 9:6); "*He was wounded for our transgressions*" (*Isaiah* 53:5); and *"I saw the Lord high and lifted up"* (*Isaiah* 6:1). It also resonates with other ancient prophetic traditions, such as *1 Enoch's* heavenly books, *Jubilees*' angelic mediation, and the *Testaments of the Twelve Patriarchs'* messianic hope and expectation of a coming Everlasting High Priest, King and Redeemer.

The Vision/Ascension of Isaiah draws readers upward with the prophet as he ascends through the layered heavens beholding The Beloved in glory and the ordered ranks of the angelic hosts. His ascent mirrors the pattern first established with Moses: entering the presence of the Most High, standing within the divine council, receiving revelation face to face and returning with words entrusted for generations yet to come.

This ascent that Isaiah experiences parallels other ancient heavenly journeys: Enoch's journeys through the heavens, Ezekiel's throne-vision, Daniel's vision of the Ancient of Days, Paul's ascent to the third heaven, and Abraham's heavenly vision, and other visions of other prophets. Isaiah's ascent is unique in its focus on the identity and mission of The Beloved. At the highest heaven, Isaiah beholds The Beloved – the pre-existent Son, radiant with divine glory, worshiped by angels, and united with the Father and the Spirit. This portrayal aligns closely with the New Testament:

> *"In the beginning was the Word, and the Word was with God, and the Word was God. The same was in the beginning with God." – John 1:1-2*

Interestingly, The Hebrew Gospels Hebrew (*see weblinks in the Resources of the After Matter*) translation gives a different view of these verses:

> *"In the beginning was the Son of Eloah. The Son of El was both with El, and the Son of El was Eloah. This one was in the beginning with El." (*Eloah and El are singular for Elohim, usually translated as 'God'. It is a later scribal translational decision to use "Word" for "El").*
>
> *"He existed in the form of יהוה/Yahweh" (Philippians 2:6), "Through whom He made the worlds" (Hebrews 1:2) and "Before Abraham was, I am." – John 8:58*

Isaiah's ascent and seeing The Beloved resonates with extracanonical visions such as *1 Enoch's* Son of Man, *Ezra*'s Man from the Sea, and *Baruch's* Coming One.

The text describes the war against Belial, the ruler of this world, who seeks to destroy The Beloved. Isaiah witnesses the schemes of the evil one, the deception of earthly rulers, and the attempt to thwart the Messiah's mission. This cosmic conflict echoes Isaiah's own prophecy of the fallen one, Daniel's visions of spiritual warfare, the war in heaven in *Revelation*, the account of Mastema in *Jubilees*, and *1 Enoch*'s portrayal of the Watchers and the destruction caused by their teachings and the influence of their offspring.

After His death, The Beloved ascends again through the heavens, now revealed in glory. The angels who did not recognize Him during His descent now worship Him as He returns victorious. This ascent mirrors the resurrection, the ascension, the exaltation of יֵשׁוּעַ/Yeshua, and the proclamation of victory over the powers. Extracanonical parallels include Enoch's exaltation of the Son of Man, Levi's exalted priest, Abraham's triumphant One, and Baruch's restoration of the righteous.

3. Authentication of *Vision/Ascension of Isaiah*

Early assemblies following יֵשׁוּעַ/Yeshua cherished *Vision/Ascension of Isaiah* because it unveiled the Messiah's pre-existence, His deliberate descent through the heavens, and the cosmic opposition that sought to hinder His mission. In Isaiah's vision – and in the stark contrast between Hezekiah's fidelity and Manasseh's betrayal – they recognized the unbroken continuity of the prophetic calling: those who stood where Moses stood saw what Moses saw, and they faithfully wrote what they were shown.

The ancient testimony surrounding *The Vision, Ascension* and *Martyrdom of Isaiah* affirms the writing's authenticity and reveals how it was preserved within Israel's historic and prophetic heritage. It is a powerful prophetic writing preserved from the ancient world long before the formalizing and binding of the Biblical canon. Isaiah's martyrdom, however, did not silence his testimony.

The historical testimony concerning *Vision/Ascension of Isiaah* is reflected in the following ancient sources, which bear witness to its reception and use:

"Isaiah was sawn in two, as you know, for speaking boldly in the Spirit." – Justin Martyr – Dialogue with Trypho 120

"Of the prophets, Isaiah endured being sawn asunder, that he might not speak contrary to the law of God." – Tertullian – Scorpiace 8

"In the Ascension of Isaiah it is shown how the prophet was taken up and what he saw in the heavens." – Origen, Commentary on Matthew 13.57

"They make use of the Ascension of Isaiah, saying that he saw the heavens opened and the Beloved descending." – Epiphanius, Panarion 40.2.5

"It is related that Isaiah was sawn asunder under Manasseh, as the Jews also hand down in their writings." – Jerome, Commentary on Isaiah 64.2

"Isaiah was sawn asunder by the people, for the truth's sake." – Apostolic Constitutions 5.20

4. Edifying Value of *Vision/Ascension of Isaiah* for the Modern Reader

Seen through this lens, the content of the *Vision/Ascension of Isaiah* reveals its enduring prophetic value and its contribution to the wider Biblical witness and the modern believer's understanding of the intent of the Divine revelation. *Vision/Ascension of Isaiah* illuminates themes central to the New Testament: the pre-existence of יְשׁוּעַ/Yeshua, the incarnation as a hidden descent, the cosmic last days battle against evil, and the Divine exaltation of the Messiah. A thoughtful reading of *Vision/Ascension of Isaiah* will unveil its striking harmony with the last-days prophecies echoed in *Revelation* and in all the prophets who came before.

TWO-FOLD WITNESS:
HOW VISION/ASCENSION OF ISAIAH AFFIRMS AND IS AFFIRMED BY OTHER PROPHETIC WITNESSES

Essential Content From *The Vision/Ascension Of Isaiah* Affirming The Biblical Authors' Declarations And Teachings:

- Isaiah's ascent through the heavens illuminates New Testament heavenly-ascent motifs in *2 Corinthians* 12 and *Revelation* 4, while paralleling earlier ascent traditions in *1 Enoch, Testament of Levi*, and the *Apocryphon of Abraham.*
- The Beloved's descent and ascent clarify the understanding of early followers of יְשׁוּעַ/Yeshua of incarnation and exaltation reflected in *Philippians* 2 and resonates with the Son of Man traditions in *1 Enoch* and the heavenly-descent imagery in *John* 1 and *Ephesians* 4.
- Angelic orders and heavenly liturgy deepen the imagery of *Isaiah* 6 and *Revelation* 4–5, harmonizing with the angelic hierarchies in *1 Enoch, Jubilees,* and the *Testament of Levi.*
- The ancient writing *Ascension, Vision and Martyrdom of Isaiah* explains the tradition referenced in *Hebrews* 11:37 ("sawn in two"), confirming early Jewish memory and the memory preserved within the assemblies of יְשׁוּעַ/Yeshua of prophetic suffering.

Additional Ancient Writings Confirming These Themes:

- *1 Enoch* (heavenly ascent, angelic orders, divine judgment, Son of Man imagery)
- Early ascent traditions from the assemblies of יְשׁוּעַ/Yeshua (e.g., *Shepherd of Hermas, Apocalypse of Peter, Apocalypse of Paul*)
- *Testament of Levi* (seven heavens, angelic ranks, priestly revelation)
- *Apocryphon of Abraham* (heavenly ascent, angelic mediation, divine throne)
- *2 Enoch* (multiple heavens, angelic hierarchies, visionary transformation)
- *Book of the Watchers* (heavenly court, judgment scenes, angelic rebellion)
- *Book of Giants* (heavenly visions, prophetic warnings)
- *Ecclesiasticus/Sirach* 48 (praise of Isaiah's prophetic authority and heavenly insight)

New Testament Writings Resonating With These Themes:

- *Matthew* 3 and *Luke* 3 (heaven opened, Spirit descending, heavenly affirmation)
- *John* 1 (the Son descending and ascending, heavenly revelation)
- *Acts* 7 (heaven opened, divine throne, martyrdom imagery)
- *2 Corinthians* 12 (Paul's ascent to the "third heaven")
- *Ephesians* 4 (the One who descended is the One who ascended above all heavens)
- *Hebrews* 1–2 (angelic hierarchy, Son's superiority, heavenly revelation)
- *Revelation* 1, 4–5, and 12 (heavenly throne room, angelic liturgy, cosmic conflict)

Ezekiel

The Exiled Watchman Who Saw Visions of Resurrection, Judgment, and Renewal

"And the Lord raised me up, and I beheld the Son of Man coming with the hosts of heaven, and the righteous who had slept were awakened to behold His glory." – Apocryphon of Ezekiel, Fragment 1 or A

"For the Son of Man shall come in the glory of His Father with His angels." – Matthew 16:27

"And Enoch also, the seventh from Adam, prophesied of these, saying, Behold, the Lord cometh with ten thousands of his saints, To execute judgment upon all, and to convince all that are ungodly among them of all their ungodly deeds which they have ungodly committed, and of all their hard speeches which ungodly sinners have spoken against him." – Jude 14–15

"And the Chosen One shall sit on the throne of glory, and the righteous dead shall arise from their sleep." – 1 Enoch 51

"For my Son the Messiah shall be revealed… and those who remain shall rejoice, and the dead shall be raised." – 2 Esdras 7:28–32

The Apocryphon of Ezekiel, attributed to Ezekiel and situated within early Jewish history, offers insight into resurrection hope, divine justice, and the restoration of God's people.

1. Ezekiel

With its authenticity established, the text invites us to consider the prophet himself and the way his voice is revealed. Although attributed to

Ezekiel, the surviving material reflects the work of later writers who preserved and transmitted Ezekielic visions. These scribes revered Ezekiel's prophetic authority and carried forward traditions that interpreted his imagery as revealing the resurrection of the righteous, the judgment of the wicked, and the restoration of creation.

2. Extracanonical Attributed to Ezekiel

The *Apocryphon of Ezekiel* is an ancient work that expands the prophet's end-time themes rather than retelling his canonical book. Preserving the same resurrection, judgment, and end-time restoration themes that characterize the Apocryphon of Ezekiel, this writing reveals how ancient believers understood Ezekiel's visions as pointing beyond the return from exile to the final consummation of all things. In these expanded scenes, the valley of dry bones becomes a literal promise of resurrection, the return of divine glory signals the world's ultimate restoration, and reminds people of the judgment of the nations in anticipation of the Great Day when evil is overthrown. Its imagery aligns with Isaiah 24–27, Daniel 12, 1 Enoch, and Revelation, demonstrating that themes central to the New Testament – resurrection, judgment, the renewal of creation, and the triumph of יהוה/Yahweh's kingdom – were already embedded in Israel's prophetic path.

3. Authentication of *Apocryphon of Ezekiel*

The ancient testimony surrounding this writing affirms its authenticity and reveals how it was preserved within Israel's prophetic heritage and is reflected in the following ancient sources, which bear witness to its reception and use:

> *"The dead shall rise, and those who are in the tombs shall be raised, and those who are in the earth shall rejoice." – Apocryphon of Ezekiel, Fragment in Epiphanius, Panarion 64.70.6*
>
> *"A father shall be judged with his son, and a son with his father, each according to his works." – Apocryphon of Ezekiel, Quoted in Clement of Alexandria, Stromata 6.16*

"The Lord will give life to the bones of the dead, clothing them with flesh and sinews." – Apocryphon of Ezekiel, Quoted in Hippolytus, On the Resurrection 2

"The prophet Ezekiel spoke of the resurrection, as also is written in the Apocryphon attributed to him." – Origen, Commentary on Matthew 27.52 (3rd century)

"They cite the book called the Apocryphon of Ezekiel, saying that the dead will rise and be judged." – Epiphanius, Panarion 64.70.6 (4th century)

"Some bring forward the Apocryphon of Ezekiel, which speaks of the resurrection of the dead." – Jerome, Commentary on Ezekiel 37 (4th century)

Fragments of an Ezekielic composition were recovered at Qumran (4Q383–4Q391), and their physical characteristics strongly support the authenticity and antiquity of the witness they preserve. These manuscripts were found in the same caves that yielded the earliest known copies of *Isaiah, Psalms, Deuteronomy*, and other Biblical books, and they share the same material features: hand-copied Hebrew script, parchment consistent with Temple scribal practices, and the characteristic deterioration patterns of scrolls stored for centuries in the Judean desert. Their discovery among the Dead Sea Scrolls places this Ezekielic writing firmly within the literary world of that period, demonstrating that it circulated alongside other prophetic and apocalyptic texts treasured by those of the Qumran community.

4. Edifying Value of *Apocryphon of Ezekiel* for the Modern Reader

Seen through this lens, the content of *Apocryphon of Ezekiel* reveals its enduring prophetic value and its contribution to the wider Biblical witness and the modern believer's understanding of the intent of the Divine revelation. For modern readers, this work stands as another witness to the continuity of hope across centuries, showing that the promise of restoration and the victory of righteousness were long understood as part of the prophetic story that יֵשׁוּעַ/Yeshua and the apostles proclaimed.

TWO-FOLD WITNESS:
HOW *APOCRYPHON OF EZEKIEL* AFFIRMS AND IS AFFIRMED BY OTHER PROPHETIC WITNESSES

Essential Content From The *Apocryphon Of Ezekiel* Paralleling Biblical Declarations:

- The resurrection vision – *Daniel* 12, *John* 5, and *1 Corinthians* 15.
- The defeat of Gog – *Revelation* 19–20.
- The restored temple – *Revelation* 21–22.
- The renewal of creation – *Isaiah* 65–66 and *Romans* 8.
- The return of divine glory – *Exodus, Ezekiel* 1, and *Revelation* 4.

Additional Ancient Writings Supporting Ezekiel's Themes:

- *1 Enoch* (resurrection, judgment, heavenly temple)
- *Jubilees* (restoration and covenant renewal)
- *Testament of Levi* (heavenly priesthood)
- Book of the Watchers (heavenly court)
- *Book of Noah* (renewal after judgment)
- *Testament of Judah* (messianic kingship)
- *Wisdom of Solomon* (immortality of the righteous)

New Testament Confirmation of Ezekiel's Themes:

- *John* 5 (resurrection)
- *Romans* 8 (creation renewed)
- *1 Corinthians* 15 (immortality)
- *Revelation* 20–22 (judgment, new creation, divine glory)

✦✧✦

Baruch

The Faithful Scribe Preserving Jeremiah's Prophetic Legacy

"Then Jeremiah called Baruch son of Neriah, and Baruch wrote on a scroll at Jeremiah's dictation all the words of the LORD that he had spoken to him." – Jeremiah 36:4

""They asked Baruch, 'Tell us, how did you write all these words? Was it at his dictation?' Baruch answered them, 'He dictated all these words to me, and I wrote them with ink on the scroll.'" – Jeremiah 36:17-18

"The Holy One does not abandon His people, but remembers the covenant in every generation." – Prayer of Azariah 2, the (Septuagint)

"The righteous who endure sorrow in this age will shine when the Ancient of Days restores His kingdom." – 4 Ezra or 2 Esdras 7:97

"Those who keep the commandments of the Lord (יהוה/Yahweh) will find mercy in the day when He gathers His scattered ones." – Ecclesiasticus/Sirach 16:14

The writings attributed to Baruch and situated within exilic and post-exilic tradition, the scribe of Jeremiah, offer insight into exile, repentance, and the enduring hope of restoration.

1. Baruch

The text of the writings of Baruch invites us to consider the prophet and scribe Baruch himself and the manner in which his voice is presented, revealed and revered. Jeremiah explicitly identifies Baruch as his scribe, noting that Baruch wrote '*all the words of the LORD*' at the prophet's dictation (*Jerimiah* 36:4, 17–18, 32), a role further confirmed by Baruch's preservation of legal documents (*Jeremiah* 32:12–16) and the personal oracle addressed to him in *Jeremiah* 45. *The Words of Baruch* portray Baruch as a prophetic interpreter who carried Jeremiah's message into the exilic and post-exilic generations.

Baruch and his writings are often overlooked in the canonical texts, Baruch being remembered only as Jeremiah's scribe – yet the ancient *Words of Baruch* reveal a far more significant figure. He was not merely a recorder of Jeremiah's words but a prophetic voice in his own right – one who bore the weight of Jerusalem's fall, the ache of exile, and the covenantal hope of restoration. *The Words of Baruch* portrays him as a shepherd of the remnant. The apocalyptic writings attributed to Baruch expand his message into sweeping visions of the last days.

2. The Writings Of Baruch

The ancient collection known as *The Words of Baruch* (in Hebrew – *Divrei Barukh*), along with the *Letter of Jeremiah* (Hebrew – *Iggeret Yirmeyahu*) and the apocalyptic writings attributed to him, expands our understanding of the prophetic mission of Baruch, Jeremiah's scribe, and illuminates the spiritual world of the exilic age. Texts found within the Dead Sea Scrolls reflect his emphasis on covenant renewal and faithfulness. The *Book of Baruch* is accompanied by the *Letter of Jeremiah*, a text preserved in the Septuagint (LXX) and the 1611 KJV Apocrypha, included in the Latin Vulgate (LV), and actual manuscript fragments in Greek were found among the Dead Sea Scrolls (DSS), and was interestingly missing from the Masoretic Text (MT).

The writings attributed to Baruch – later labeled *1 Baruch, 2 Baruch*, and the *Letter of Jeremiah* – preserve the theological heartbeat of Jeremiah's ministry: confession, lament, repentance, and the assurance of יהוה/Yahweh's covenant mercy. These texts wrestle with the destruction of Jerusalem, the problem of evil, the hope of resurrection, and the coming of the Messiah, placing Baruch among the most significant voices of end times prophecy.

3. Authentication of Baruch's Writings

The ancient historical testimony surrounding Baruch's writings affirm their authenticity and reveals how they were preserved within Israel's prophetic heritage and are reflected in the following ancient sources, which bear witness to the writings of Baruch and their reception and use:

> *"Baruch read the words of this book in the hearing of Jeconiah son of Jehoiakim king of Judah." – Septuagint, Baruch 1:3*
>
> *"Thus says the Lord Almighty, the God of Israel: 'You shall read this book which Baruch wrote at my dictation.'" – Letter of Jeremiah, Baruch 6:1*
>
> *"After the destruction of the city, Baruch sat weeping and lamenting, saying, 'O Lord, why have You set fire to Your vineyard?'" – 2 Baruch 1:1*
>
> *"Baruch, the scribe of Jeremiah, wrote many things in the book that bears his name." – Josephus, Antiquities 10.9.1*
>
> *"Jeremiah commanded Baruch, who also wrote the things that were read to the people." – 4 Ezra/2 Esdras 14:24*
>
> *"Baruch also prophesied after Jeremiah, and his book is read among us." – Origen, Homilies on Jeremiah 1.1*
>
> *"Jeremiah and Baruch taught the people in Babylon, as is written in the book of Baruch." – Origen, Commentary on Isaiah 64.2*
>
> *"Some read the Book of Baruch with Jeremiah, though it is not in the Hebrew canon." – Jerome, Prologue to Jeremiah lines 20–23*
>
> *"The Letter of Jeremiah is placed with Baruch, and is read in the churches." – Athanasiu, Festal Letter 39*
>
> *"Baruch, who wrote the words of Jeremiah, left also his own book, which some include with the prophet." – Cyril of Jerusalem, Catechetical Lecture 4.35*
>
> *"The book of Baruch is useful for instruction, though not counted among the canonical books." – Augustine, On Christian Doctrine 2.8*

4. Edifying Value the Writings of Baruch for the Modern Reader

Viewed within this framework, the content of the writings and words of Baruch reveal their enduring prophetic value and its contribution to the wider Biblical witness and the modern believer's understanding of the intent of the Divine revelation. The apocalyptic writings labeled *1 Baruch* and *2 Baruch* are included in the ancient Jewish end time texts for that era. Baruch's revelations concerning the rise and fall of empires, the suffering of the righteous, the testing of Israel, the coming of the Messiah, the resurrection of the dead, the final judgment, and the restoration of creation place The Words of Baruch, Daniel, Ezra/Esdras, the later apocalyptic seers, and the visions of Revelation invite every follower of יֵשׁוּעַ/Yeshua into a deeper understanding of the prophetic hope of the last days.

———— ✦✧✦ ————

TWO-FOLD WITNESS:
HOW BARUCH'S WRITINGS AFFIRM AND
ARE AFFIRMED BY OTHER PROPHETIC WITNESSES

Essential Content From Baruch's Writings Confirming The Biblical Authors' Declarations And Teachings:

- *1 Baruch* reinforces themes of repentance, confession, and restoration found in *Deuteronomy* 30, *Nehemiah* 9, and *Daniel* 9.
- *2 Baruch* reflects judgment, hope, and restoration paralleling *Jeremiah, Lamentations, Daniel* 9, and *Revelation* 6–8.
- *1 Enoch* parallels *Baruch's* themes of judgment, resurrection, and renewal, reflected in *Matthew* 24, *1 Thessalonians* 4–5, and *Revelation* 20–22.
- *Jubilees* supports *Baruch's* emphasis on repentance, obedience, and national restoration, aligning with *Genesis, Deuteronomy,* and *Isaiah* 40–66.

Additional Ancient Writings Supporting *Baruch's* Themes:

- *4 Ezra:* justice; suffering; fate of the righteous.
- The Dead Sea Scrolls: exile; judgment; covenant renewal; heavenly books; eschatological hope.
- *Testament of Levi* (heavenly tablets, priestly revelation, and judgment)
- *Testament of Judah* (messianic expectation and the rise of the righteous)
- *Apocryphon of Abraham* (heavenly ascent, divine judgment, and covenant renewal)
- *Ecclesiasticus/Sirach* 36–50 (praise of Israel's leaders, covenant memory, and hope for restoration)
- *Wisdom of Solomon* (vindication of the righteous, divine justice, and the fate of the wicked)

New Testament Writings Resonating With *Baruch's* Prophetic And Eschatological Themes:

- *Matthew* 23–24 (judgment on Jerusalem, prophetic lament, and the coming age)
- *Luke* 21 (destruction of the Temple and the hope of redemption)
- *Romans* 9–11 (Israel's exile, remnant theology, and future restoration)

- *2 Corinthians* 4–5 (suffering, renewal, and the unseen heavenly reality)
- *Hebrews* 11 (endurance, exile, and the hope of a better country)
- *Revelation* 6–11 (judgment; heavenly visions; righteous vindication)

Esdras/Ezra

Witnesses to Israel's Restoration and the Sovereignty of God

"The Most High gave understanding to the five men, and they wrote by night what was spoken by day." – 2 Esdras 14:42

"Bind up the testimony; seal the teaching among My disciples." – Isaiah 8:16

"Write the things which you have seen and heard, for they are appointed for the last days." – Apocryphon of Abraham 31

"Write the vision; make it plain on tablets, so he may run who reads it." – Habakkuk 2:2

"All Scripture is breathed out by God (יהוה/Yahweh) and profitable for teaching, for reproof, for correction, and for training in righteousness." – 2 Timothy 3:16

The Books of Esdras, attributed to Ezra and situated within post-exilic Hebrew literature, offer insight into temple restoration, covenant renewal, and the shaping of Israel's identity after return.

1. The Prophet and Scribe Ezra also called Ezdras

The text of Ezra's writings invites us to consider the prophet Ezra – also called Esdras – and the way his voice is presented, received, revered, and preserved. Esdras is the Greek form of the name Ezra, the same prophetic scribe credited with the authorship of *Ezra, 1* and *2 Ezdras, 1* and *2 Chronicles* and the compiler of *Nehemiah.*

Ezra stood at the heart of Israel's restoration. A priest, scribe, and teacher of the Law, he led the returned exiles not only in rebuilding their community but in recovering their covenant identity. His mission was one of spiritual reconstruction – renewing covenant faithfulness through the reading, teaching, and preservation of Scripture. He taught the Law to a generation born in exile and reestablished covenant worship among the restored community.

Ancient tradition remembers him as a "second Moses," a prophet-scribe who ensured that the Scriptures remained central to Israel's life after the destruction of Jerusalem.

2. The Extracanonical Writings Of Ezra

The writings known as *1 Esdras* and *2 Esdras* preserve two distinct but complementary strands of the Ezra tradition – one historical and restorative, the other visionary and apocalyptic.

1 Esdras retells and expands the restoration narrative found in *2 Chronicles, Ezra,* and *Nehemiah.* It opens with the fall of Jerusalem, recounts the decree of Cyrus, and follows the return of the exiles as they rebuild the temple and restore worship. The text preserves the "Three Guardsmen" account – a wisdom contest before King Darius that culminates in the recognition of truth and the advancement of Zerubbabel. This narrative, absent from the Masoretic Text, highlights divine sovereignty, the triumph of truth, and the legitimacy of the restoration leadership. *1 Esdras* concludes with the public reading of the Law, emphasizing Ezra's role as priest, scribe, and teacher.

2 Esdras (also called *4 Ezra*) presents a different dimension of Ezra's legacy. Composed after the destruction of Jerusalem, it records Ezra's dialogues with יהוה/Yahweh concerning suffering, justice, and the fate of Israel. The writing is structured around a series of visions – the mourning woman transformed into the restored Jerusalem, the eagle representing oppressive kingdoms, and the man rising from the sea who brings deliverance. The final chapters portray Ezra receiving, dictating, and restoring sacred writings that had been lost, echoing ancient tradition that he reestablished the Scriptures for the post-exilic community. In this way, *2 Esdras* preserves both the anguish and the hope of a people seeking understanding after catastrophe.

3. Authentication of Esdras/Ezra's Extracanonical Writings

The ancient testimony surrounding these writings affirms their authenticity and reveals how they were preserved within Israel's prophetic heritage. Esdras is simply the Greek rendering of the name Ezra, referring to the same scribe and prophet.

After the exile, the recovery of sacred history became essential, for many prophetic and priestly writings had been seized, burned, or lost during the Babylonian destruction of Jerusalem (*Jeremiah* 36:23, 27–28, 32; *2 Kings* 25:9, 13–17; *2 Chronicles* 36:18–19; *Ezra* 4:15; *1 Esdras* 1–2; *2 Esdras* 14:21–22, 45–48). Under Ezra's leadership, the scribes gathered, ordered, and safeguarded the prophetic writings so that the voice of יהוה/Yahweh would not fade amid the dust of Babylon (*Ezra* 7:6, 10–11, 14, 21; *Nehemiah* 8:1–8; 9:3; *2 Chronicles* 36:18–19; *1 Esdras* 1–2; *2 Esdras* 14:19–22, 38–48).

The historical testimony concerning the extracanonical writings of *Ezra/Esdras* is reflected in the following ancient sources, which bear witness to their existence, reception and use:

> *"Let us turn to the words of Esdras, who testifies that the righteous shall shine and receive the reward prepared for them." – Irenaeus, Against Heresies 5.35*

> *"As Esdras says, after the times of sorrow the righteous shall receive the glory laid up for them." – Cyprian, Testimonia 2.22*

> *"Esdras also teaches concerning the resurrection and the ordering of the age to come." – Ambrose, On the Good of Death 10.45*

> *"Some of the books, such as Esdras, are read in the churches, though they are not placed among the canonical writings." – Athanasius, Festal Letter 39*

> *"Esdras is handed down among the ancient writings, and many have preserved it in the churches." – Augustine, City of God 20.25*

The Septuagint (LXX) preserves a broader collection of Hebrew writings than the later Masoretic Text, and the 1611 KJV includes *2 Esdras,* yet modern Bibles do not.

The ancient "*Book of Ezra*" and the writings later labeled *1* and *2 Esdras* unveil the struggles, visions, and divine instruction that shaped the restored community and carried forward Ezra's prophetic legacy.

4. Edifying Value of Ezra/Esdras' Extracanonical Writings for the Modern Reader

Seen through this lens, the content of *1* and *2 Esdras* reveals enduring prophetic value and contributes to the wider Biblical witness and the modern believer's understanding of the intent of the Divine revelation.

2 Esdras is one of the most important Jewish apocalyptic texts. Composed in the wake of Jerusalem's destruction, it wrestles with the deepest questions of suffering, justice, and the end of the age. Ezra's dialogues with יהוה/*Yahweh* echo the laments of Job and the questions of Jeremiah, yet they move toward restoration hope. He is shown symbolic visions – an eagle representing oppressive kingdoms, a man rising from the sea, and a restored Jerusalem descending in glory. These visions shaped early Jewish eschatology and the eschatology of the followers of י_שוע_/Yeshua and appear again in the teachings of י_שוע_/Yeshua, the letters of Paul, and the prophetic *Book of Revelation* penned by John.

———— ✦✧✦ ————

TWO-FOLD WITNESS:
HOW EZRA/ESDRAS' EXTRACANONICAL WRITINGS AFFIRM AND ARE AFFIRMED BY OTHER PROPHETIC WITNESSES

Essential Content From Ezra/Esdras' Writings That Parallel The Biblical Authors' Declarations And Teachings:

- *1 Esdras* preserves expanded accounts of Israel's return from exile, illuminating the spiritual, political, and communal challenges behind *Ezra–Nehemiah* retells of the rebuilding of the Temple and the restoration of worship parallels themes in *Haggai, Zechariah*, and the covenant-renewal scenes of *Deuteronomy* 30 and *Nehemiah* 8–10.
- *2 Esdras* (also known as *4 Ezra*) explores prophetic questions about suffering, divine justice, and the end of the age, paralleling the apocalyptic wrestling of *Daniel* 7–12 and the visionary sequences of *Revelation* 6–22. Its laments over Jerusalem echo *Lamentations*, while its visions of the Son of Man resonate with *1 Enoch* and *Matthew* 24.
- *Jubilees* provides covenantal and chronological frameworks that clarify *Esdras'* emphasis on restoration, obedience, and sacred time. Its genealogical precision and heavenly-tablet traditions reinforce the restoration theology found in *Ezra, Nehemiah*, and the prophetic hope of *Isaiah* 40–66.
- *1 Enoch* deepens the eschatological imagery found in *2 Esdras*, especially concerning judgment, resurrection, and the coming age. Its visions of the righteous remnant, the fate of the wicked, and the unveiling of the final kingdom parallel New Testament themes in *Matthew* 25, *1 Thessalonians* 4–5, and *Revelation* 20–22.

Ancient Writings That Support Ezra/Esdras' Themes:

- The Dead Sea Scrolls (apocalyptic reflections on restoration, divine justice, covenant renewal, and the identity of the faithful remnant, paralleling the concerns of *2 Esdras* and the prophetic hope of *Isaiah, Jeremiah*, and *Daniel*)
- *Testament of Levi* (priestly authority, heavenly revelation, and covenant renewal)
- *Apocryphon of Abraham* (heavenly ascent, divine judgment, and the fate of nations)

- *Ecclesiasticus/Sirach* 36–50 (praise of Israel's leaders, Temple restoration, and covenant memory)
- *Wisdom of Solomon* (divine justice, vindication of the righteous, and the destiny of the wicked)
- *1* and *2 Baruch* (lament over Jerusalem, hope for restoration, and eschatological expectation)
- Josephus' *Antiquities* provides historical expansions of the return from exile, political tensions, and priestly leadership that illuminate the background of *Ezra–Nehemiah* and *1 Esdras.*

New Testament Writings Resonating With Ezra/Esdras' Themes:

- *Matthew* 24–25 (judgment, the coming age, and the fate of the righteous and wicked)
- *Luke* 1–3 (genealogies, restoration hope, and prophetic fulfillment)
- *Acts* 1–3 (restoration of Israel, prophetic witness, and divine justice)
- *Romans* 9–11 (remnant theology, exile, and future restoration)
- *Hebrews* 12 (heavenly Jerusalem, divine discipline, and covenant renewal)
- *Revelation* 6–11 (judgment, heavenly visions, and the vindication of the faithful)

✦✧✦

Ecclesiasticus/Sirach

The Fear of the Lord as the Root of Wisdom

"Wisdom exalts her children and lays hold of those who seek her." – Ecclesiasticus/Sirach 4:11

"The fear of the Lord is the beginning of wisdom, and knowledge of the Holy One is insight." – Proverbs 9:10

"Give your heart to instruction and your ears to words of understanding." – 4QInstruction (Dead Sea Scrolls)

"If any of you lacks wisdom, let him ask God (יהוה/Yahweh), who gives generously to all without reproach." – James 1:5

"Draw near to me, you who are uneducated, and lodge in the house of instruction." – Ecclesiasticus/Sirach 51:23

Ecclesiasticus also known as Sirach, composed by Jesus ben Sirach or Ben Sira, offers insight into wisdom, virtue, and the practical shaping of a life rooted in reverence for God.

1. Jesus ben Sirach or Ben Sira

The text of *Ecclesiasticus/Sirach* invites us to consider the author Jesus ben Sirach and the manner in which his voice is presented, preserved, received, revered. Ben Sira writes as a sage, a teacher, and a father instructing his sons. His voice is pastoral yet authoritative, steeped in Scripture yet attentive to the pressures of Hellenistic culture. Through him we glimpse a Judaism fiercely committed to covenant faithfulness while navigating the complexities of empire, assimilation, and identity. Ben Sira's world is one in which Scripture saturates daily life. His teachings assume a people shaped by covenant memory, prophetic expectation, and the hope of divine intervention.

Sirach's grandson's prologue, one of the earliest reflections on translation in Jewish literature, reveals how beloved this book already was in his own day. He translated it into Greek "for those living abroad," ensuring that diaspora communities could inherit the same wisdom that continually strengthened Jerusalem's faithful.

2. *Ecclesiasticus/Sirach*

Its themes echo through the teachings of יְשׁוּעַ/Yeshua, the letter of *James,* the *Didache*, and the writings of the earliest bishops. Its ethical instructions, warnings against hypocrisy, exaltation of humility, and celebration of divine wisdom form a bridge between the prophets and the apostles – a living stream of instruction flowing into the 1st century.

Ecclesiasticus/Sirach opens a window into the spiritual atmosphere of pre-Messianic Judaism:

- Wisdom as a living, active presence calling and guiding.
- Torah as the center of life
- Humility as the path to honor
- Repentance as the doorway to restoration
- The fear of יהוה/Yahweh as the beginning of wisdom
- The righteous community as the guardian of tradition

3. Authentication of *Ecclesiasticus/Sirach*

The historic testimony surrounding *Ecclesiasticus/Sirach* affirms its authenticity and reveals how it was preserved within Israel's prophetic heritage and is reflected in the following ancient sources, which bear witness to its reception and use:

> *"Many great teachings have been given to us through the Law and the Prophets, and through others who followed after them." – Prologue to Sirach (grandson of Ben Sira), Greek Prologue*

> *"Have you not read the writings of the wise, such as the words of Jesus son of*

Sirach?" – Dead Sea Scrolls (Ben Sira fragments), Masada Scrolls

"As also the Scripture says: 'Do not praise a man before he speaks,' which is found in the book of Jesus son of Sirach." – Clement of Alexandria, Stromata 2.23

"The book of Jesus son of Sirach is full of wise instruction and is read in the churches." – Origen, Homilies on Joshua 15.6

"Ecclesiasticus, which is also called the Wisdom of Jesus son of Sirach, is among the books read for edification." – Origen, Commentary on Romans 3.6

"The Church reads the book of Sirach for the instruction of catechumens." – Apostolic Constitutions 6.14

"Jesus son of Sirach wrote a book full of virtue and wisdom, which the Church indeed reads, though it is not in the Hebrew canon." – Jerome, Prologue to the Books of Solomon

"Ecclesiasticus is appointed to be read for the instruction of those newly joining us." – Athanasius, Festal Letter 39

"Sirach, though not in the Hebrew canon, is held in honor and read in the Church for the instruction of the faithful." – Cyril of Jerusalem, Catechetical Lecture 4.35

"The book of Ecclesiasticus is useful for the instruction of manners and the cultivation of virtue." – Augustine, On Christian Doctrine 2.8

"Jesus son of Sirach, a wise man, wrote a book which many of the Fathers commend." – Cassiodorus, Institutiones 1.1

Ecclesiasticus/Sirach is remarkably interesting as it is preserved in the Septuagint and the Latin Vulgate, absent from the Masoretic Text, and attested in Hebrew fragments among the Dead Sea Scrolls. Written in Hebrew around 180 BCE by Yeshua ben Sira and translated into Greek by his grandson a generation later, this book bridges the world of *Proverbs* and the world of יֵשׁוּעַ/Yeshua the Messiah. Its teachings molded the ethical practices and thinking of Judaism, offering a portrait of righteous living rooted in Torah, humility, repentance, and the fear of יהוה/*Yahweh.*

4. Edifying Value of *Ecclesiasticus/Sirach* for the Modern Reader

Seen through this lens, the content of *Ecclesiasticus/Sirach* reveals its enduring prophetic value and its contribution to the wider Biblical witness and the modern believer's understanding of the intent of the Divine revelation.

Ecclesiasticus/Sirach's influence on the early assemblies of ־י־שוע/Yeshua is unmistakable. The early believers did not treat *Ecclesiasticus/Sirach* as a marginal text. It appears in instructional writings and reading cycles the writings of the Apostolic Fathers, the teachings of the early bishops, the ethical instruction of catechumens, and the Scriptural libraries of the earliest communities.

Ecclesiasticus/Sirach's warnings about the tongue are echoed in the *Epistle of James.* The *Two Ways* teaching is mirrored by The *Didache. Ecclesiasticus/Sirach*'s wisdom imagery resonates with ־י־שוע/Yeshua's parables. For the early assemblies, *Ecclesiasticus/Sirach* was not merely literature – it was a guide for righteous living, a companion to *Proverbs*, and a witness to the continuity of Israel's wisdom literature and edifying for the modern reader.

———— ✦✧✦ ————

TWO-FOLD WITNESS: HOW ECCLESIASTICUS/SIRACH AFFIRMS AND IS AFFIRMED BY OTHER PROPHETIC WITNESSES

Essential Content From *Ecclesiasticus/Sirach* Paralleling The Biblical Authors' Declarations And Teachings:

- *Ecclesiasticus/Sirach* preserves the wisdom tradition of Israel in the post-exilic period, echoing the ethical instruction of *Proverbs*, the humility themes of *Isaiah* 57–66, and the covenant-centered life emphasized in *Deuteronomy* 4–11.
- *Ecclesiasticus/Sirach*'s teachings on repentance, covenant faithfulness, and the fear of יהוה/Yahweh parallel the prophetic calls of *Jeremiah* 7, *Hosea* 14, and *Joel* 2, reinforcing the Biblical pattern of returning to יהוה/Yahweh with humility and obedience.
- *Ecclesiasticus/Sirach*'s praise of Israel's leaders (*Ecclesiasticus/Sirach* 44–50) mirrors the covenant memory of *Psalm* 105, *Nehemiah* 9, and the historical summaries in *Joshua* 24 and *1 Samuel* 12.
- *Ecclesiasticus/Sirach*'s warnings about the tongue, hypocrisy, and false speech align with *Psalm* 34, *Proverbs* 10–12, and the ethical demands of *Micah* 6:8.

Additional Ancient Writings Supporting *Ecclesiasticus/Sirach*:

- *Wisdom of Solomon* (divine justice, the destiny of the righteous and wicked, and the role of Wisdom in creation and revelation)
- *Testaments of the Twelve Patriarchs* (ethical exhortation, father-to-son instruction, and the contrast between covenant faithfulness and lawlessness)
- *Jubilees* (covenant memory, obedience, and the preservation of sacred tradition)
- Dead Sea Scrolls (community discipline, ethical purity, and the pursuit of righteousness in a corrupt age)
- *1 Enoch* (covenant faithfulness, judgment, and the vindication of the faithful)
- *1* and *2 Baruch* (lament, repentance, and hope for restoration)
- *Tobit* (almsgiving, righteousness, and the fear of יהוה/Yahweh)
- *Psalm of Solomon* (purity; justice; hope for a righteous king)

New Testament Writings Resonating With *Ecclesiasticus/ Sirach's* Themes:

- *Matthew* 5–7 (humility, mercy, purity of heart, and the way of righteousness)
- *Luke* 6 and 11–12 (generosity, stewardship, and the dangers of hypocrisy)
- *James* 1–3 (the tongue, endurance, humility, and the testing of faith)
- *Romans* 12 (ethical transformation, humility, and communal covenant faithfulness)
- *Hebrews* 12–13 (discipline, wisdom, and the pursuit of holiness)

Books Of The Maccabees

Testimonies of Courage, Covenant Loyalty, and Divine Deliverance

"Be strong and of a good courage, fear not, nor be afraid of them: for the LORD thy God, he it is that doth go with thee; he will not fail thee, nor forsake thee." – Deuteronomy 31:6

"And they that understand among the people shall instruct many; yet they shall fall by the sword, and by flame, by captivity, and by spoil, many days." – Daniel 11:33

"Remember the deeds of the fathers, which they did in their generations; and you shall receive great honour and an everlasting name." – 1 Maccabees 2:51 (LXX)

"Do not fear the words of a proud man, for his glory shall be dung and worms. Today he is lifted up, and tomorrow he shall be found no more." – 2 Maccabees 7:16 (LXX)

The Books of the Maccabees, attributed to early Jewish historians and situated after the exile and return from Babylon within the Hellenistic era, explore themes of faithful resistance and covenant loyalty within their ancient setting.

1. Authors

The *Books of the Maccabees* arise from within the priestly and scholarly circles of the Hasmonean era, written by those who witnessed or inherited the memory of the revolt. The authors do not identify themselves by name, yet their work reflects deep familiarity with the Temple, the priesthood, and the covenantal obligations of Israel.

1□Maccabees was composed in Hebrew, later preserved in Greek translation, and reflects the style of earlier Biblical chronicles. Its author writes with the precision of an archivist, preserving speeches, decrees, genealogies, and military accounts. Judas Maccabeus stands at the heart of this record, his campaigns forming the backbone of the narrative.

2□Maccabees, by contrast, is an abridgment of a larger five-volume history written by Jason of Cyrene (*2□Maccabees* 2:23). The epitomist writes in polished Greek, emphasizing divine intervention, prayer, martyrdom, and resurrection. His purpose is not merely to record events but to interpret them, offering a theological remembrance that strengthens the faithful and honors those who suffered for the covenant. Within this theological framing, Judas remains the chief figure through whom God's deliverance is displayed.

Together, these authors preserve the final historical movement before the arrival of the Messiah, capturing the spiritual, political, and theological tensions that shaped the world of the 1st century.

2. *Books of the Maccabees* and Their Contents

The *Books of the Maccabees* form the final historical bridge between the prophetic age and the world into which יֵשׁוּעַ/Yeshua was born. Known in Hebrew culture as *Sifrei ha-Makabim*, these writings preserve the remembrance of Israel's struggle for covenantal faithfulness during the oppression of the Seleucid Empire (see also *Daniel* 8:9–14; 11:21–35). They recount the rise of the priestly Hasmonean family, the desecration and restoration of the Temple, and the fierce devotion that ignited a national revival (*1□Maccabees* 1–4).

Although not included in the modern Hebrew canon, 1 and 2□Maccabees were faithfully preserved within Jewish communities of the ancient Hebrew world and later within the Greek-speaking synagogues of the diaspora. Their historical reliability was respected, and their remembrance of courage, martyrdom, and covenant loyalty shaped the spiritual perspective of early Judaism (see *Ecclesiasticus/Sirach* 44–50).

These books belong to the ancient category *Divrei ha-Yamim ha-Aḥaronim*, 'the later chronicles,' which preserved the final chapters of Israel's post-exilic, pre-Messianic history.

The Maccabean era marks a turning point in Israel's story. The prophetic voice had fallen silent (see *1□Maccabees* 4:46; 9:27; 14:41), yet the people's devotion had not. The persecution under Antiochus□IV forced Israel to choose between assimilation or faithfulness (*1□Maccabees* 1:41–50). Families who refused to eat unclean food (*2□Maccabees* 6:18; 7:1), who circumcised their sons (*1□Maccabees* 1:60–61), and who kept the Sabbath in secret (*1□Maccabees* 2:29–38) became the living testimony of covenant endurance (see also *Daniel* 11:32–35). Their courage prepared the spiritual landscape of the 1st century, shaping the expectations of deliverance, purity, and kingdom that appear throughout the Gospels (*Luke* 1:68–75; *John* 10:22–39).

The remembrance of martyrdom in *2□Maccabees* – including the mother and her seven sons (*2□Maccabees* 7), Eleazar the scribe (*2□Maccabees* 6:18–31), and the countless unnamed faithful – reveals a deepening belief in resurrection and Divine justice (see also *Daniel* 12:2–3; *Wisdom of Solomon* 3:1–9). These themes echo through *Daniel*, the teachings of יֵשׁוּעַ/Yeshua (*Matthew* 22:31–32; *John* 5:28–29), and the writings of Paul (*Romans* 8:18; *1□Corinthians* 15:20–26). The Maccabean martyrs became symbols of steadfastness, their stories retold in synagogues and early assemblies as examples of faith under trial (*Hebrews* 11:35–38).

The Origin of Hanukkah

The restoration of the Temple, commemorated in the festival of Hanukkah, stands as one of the most enduring legacies of this era. (*1□Maccabees* 4:52–59; *2□Maccabees* 10:1–8). The rededication of the altar, the cleansing of the sanctuary, and the renewal of worship became a sign that יהוה/Yahweh had not abandoned His people (see also *Psalm*

30:1; *Isaiah* 52:1). Even in the Gospels, the memory of this event remains alive, for יֵשׁוּעַ/Yeshua is found in the Temple during the Feast of Dedication, walking in Solomon's porch and instructing the people (*John* 10:22–23).

Covenant loyalty stands at the center of these books. The call of Mattathias, *"Whoever is zealous for the Torah, follow me"* (*1□Maccabees* 2:27), echoes the ancient command to love יהוה/*Yahweh* with all one's heart and strength (*Deuteronomy* 6:4–9). The faithful who resisted assimilation embody the enduring call to holiness. Persecution and endurance appear throughout the narrative. The oppression under Antiochus□IV mirrors the visions of Daniel (*Daniel* 7:21, 25; 11:32–35), revealing how the righteous suffer yet remain steadfast. These themes prepare the reader for the trials faced by the early assemblies (*Hebrews* 11:35–38). Deliverance and divine help are woven through both books. Prayers, victories, and miraculous interventions recall the pattern of salvation found in the Psalms and the prophets (*Psalm* 18:16–19; *1□Maccabees* 4:30–33). Resurrection hope emerges with clarity in *2□Maccabees.* The confessions of the martyrs affirm that יהוה/*Yahweh* will raise the faithful to life (*2□Maccabees* 7; *Daniel* 12:2). This hope becomes foundational in the teachings of יֵשׁוּעַ/Yeshua and the apostles (*Matthew* 22:31–32; *1□Corinthians* 15:20–26).

The sanctity of the Temple is central to both books. The cleansing and rededication of the sanctuary (*1□Maccabees* 4:36–59; *2□Maccabees* 2:19–22) affirm that worship and holiness remain at the heart of Israel's identity (*Psalm* 132:13–14). This remembrance continues into the Gospels, where the Feast of Dedication frames the teaching of יֵשׁוּעַ/Yeshua (*John* 10:22–23). *Revelation* speaks of the Temple:

> *"And there was given me a reed like unto a rod: and the angel stood, saying, Rise, and measure the temple of God, and the altar, and them that worship therein. But the court which is without the temple leave out, and measure it not; for it is given unto the Gentiles: and the holy city shall they tread under foot forty*

and two months." – Revelation 11:1-2

Interestingly, the Hebrew Gospels project's translation of the Hebrew *Book of Revelation* reveals a striking discrepancy in these verses. The difference between modern English Bibles translated from Greek and English translations made from the Hebrew text will be of particular interest to anyone who studies end-times prophecy and seeks to understand the last days:

> *"Then a reed like a rod was given to me, and he said, "Stand up, measure the temple of Yahweh, and its altar, and those who pray in it, 2 but cast out the inner temple, and do not measure it, for it is given to the nations, and they will tread down the set-apart city, forty-two months." – Revelation 11:1-2 (Hebrew Gospels Translation)*

Readers interested in this difference may explore it further on their own, and its implications are left for them to consider.

3. Authentication of the Maccabean Books

The historic testimony surrounding these writings affirms their authenticity and reveals how they were preserved within Israel's prophetic heritage and are reflected in the following ancient sources, which bear witness to its reception and use:

> *"Judas Maccabeus and his brothers purified the sanctuary and restored the altar." – Josephus, Antiquities 12.7.6*

> *"The books of the Maccabees tell how God helped those who fought for the laws." – Tertullian, Scorpiace 8*

> *"The mother and her seven sons, whose story is in the Maccabees, endured suffering for the sake of piety." – Origen, Exhortation to Martyrdom 28*

> *"The seven brothers in the Maccabees, with their mother, are an example of steadfastness." – Cyprian of Carthage, Exhortation to Martyrdom*

> *"The Church reads the Maccabees for the edification of the faithful." – Apostolic Constitutions 6.14*

> *"The books of the Maccabees are appointed to be read for the instruction of the newly baptized." – Athanasius, Festal Letter 39 (4th century)*

"The Maccabees, though not in the Hebrew canon, are read in the churches for the strengthening of faith." – Cyril of Jerusalem, Catechetical Lecture 4.35

"The books of the Maccabees are useful for the instruction of manners and the example of courage." – Augustine, City of God 18.36

4. Edifying Value for the Modern Reader

The *Books of the Maccabees* preserve the historic memory of a generation that refused to abandon covenant faithfulness in the face of persecution. Their themes resonate across the prophetic writings and the teachings of the apostles. These writings preserve the concluding chapter of Israel's pre-Messianic history, revealing the faith, courage, and hope that prepared the way for the coming of the Messiah. The *Books of the Maccabees* stand as a historic testimony to the endurance of the righteous and the faithfulness of יהוה/*Yahweh* to His covenant people (see *Malachi* 3:16–18; *Revelation* 12:17).

✦✧✦

TWO-FOLD WITNESS:
HOW THE *BOOKS OF THE MACCABEES* AFFIRM AND ARE AFFIRMED BY OTHER PROPHETIC WITNESSES

Essential Content From *1 and 2 Baruch* Paralleling The Biblical Authors' Declarations And Teachings:

- *1 Maccabees* preserves a disciplined historical account of Israel's struggle for covenant faithfulness under foreign oppression. Its themes of zeal, purification, and national restoration parallel the prophetic calls of *Haggai, Zechariah*, and the covenant renewal scenes of *Deuteronomy* 30 and *Nehemiah* 8–10. The rededication of the Temple echoes *Ezekiel's* visions of restored worship and Isaiah's hope for a purified remnant.
- *2 Maccabees* deepens the theological dimension of the Maccabean revolt, emphasizing resurrection hope, martyrdom, angelic intervention, and divine justice. Its portrayal of the righteous suffering for the covenant resonates with *Daniel* 7–12, the apocalyptic visions of *1 Enoch*, and New Testament teachings on vindication and resurrection (*Matthew* 25; *Hebrews* 11; *Revelation* 20–22).
- *Jubilees* reinforces the Maccabean emphasis on covenant fidelity, sacred time, and the preservation of Israel's identity. Its focus on purity, heavenly tablets, and obedience to ancestral commandments parallels the Maccabean defense of Torah observance and the sanctity of the Temple.
- *1 Enoch* amplifies the eschatological themes found in *2 Maccabees*, especially divine judgment, the vindication of the righteous, and the overthrow of wicked rulers. Its visions of heavenly warfare and the coming kingdom mirror the Maccabean conviction that יהוה/*Yahweh* intervenes in history to defend His faithful ones.

Additional Ancient Writings That Support Maccabean Themes:

- Josephus' *Antiquities* – historical expansions of the Hasmonean era, political tensions, priestly leadership, and the struggle for national sovereignty that undergirds *1 Maccabees.*
- Dead Sea Scrolls – reflections on persecution, covenant purity, and eschatological hope. Their emphasis on the faithful remnant, divine

justice, and the triumph of light over darkness parallels the Maccabean worldview and the apocalyptic concerns of *Daniel* and *1 Enoch*.

- *Testament of Levi* – priestly authority, heavenly revelation, and the sanctity of the priesthood, echoing the Hasmonean restoration of Temple service.
- *Apocryphon of Abraham* – heavenly ascent, divine judgment, and the fate of nations, resonating with the Maccabean understanding of יהוה/*Yahweh*'s intervention in history.
- *Ecclesiasticus/Sirach* 36–50 – praise of Israel's leaders, celebration of Temple worship, and preservation of covenant memory, aligning with the Maccabean defense of Israel's sacred institutions.
- *Wisdom of Solomon* – divine justice, vindication of the righteous, and the immortality of the faithful, paralleling the martyr theology of *2 Maccabees*.
- *1* and *2 Baruch* – lament over Jerusalem, hope for restoration, and eschatological expectation, echoing the Maccabean conviction that יהוה/Yahweh restores His people through judgment and mercy.

New Testament Writings Resonating With Maccabean Themes:

- *Matthew* 24–25 – judgment, perseverance, and the destiny of the righteous and wicked
- *Luke* 1–3 – priestly lineage, restoration hope, and prophetic fulfillment
- *Acts* 1–3 – restoration of Israel, divine intervention, and the witness of the faithful
- *Romans* 9–11 – remnant theology, covenant identity, and future restoration
- *Hebrews* 11–12 – the faith of the martyrs, divine discipline, and the heavenly reward
- *Revelation* 6–11 – heavenly warfare, judgment, and the vindication of יהוה/*Yahweh*'s faithful ones

FIFTH ERA:

Teachings Of יֵשׁוּעַ/Yeshua And The Apostles

The Apostolic Authors

From Beyond The Canon, The Apostles' Teachings, Lives, Acts And Deaths

"And from Levi and Judah shall arise those who teach all the nations, shining forth as lights in the world."
– Testament of Levi 14

"And I saw the Twelve Apostles standing with the Beloved, and their garments were brighter than the sun." – Vision/Ascension of Isaiah 9

"Hold fast to the practices you received from us, whether by word or by letter." – 2 Thessalonians 2:15

"The apostles received the gospel for us from the Lord Jesus Christ (יֵשׁוּעַ/Yeshua); Jesus the Christ was sent forth from God (יהוה/Yahweh)." – 1 Clement 42

"So the apostles and teachers who preached the name of the Son of God (יהוה/Yahweh) walked in the power and great glory of the Lord." – Shepherd of Hermas, Vision 3 (Similitude 3), Chapter 5

The writings associated with the Apostolic Authors, situated within the first-century assemblies, offer insight into early teaching and community formation within the assemblies of יֵשׁוּעַ/Yeshua, and the transmission of the Messiah's message. Together, the established Scriptures and the wider memorials reveal the depth and richness of the apostolic heritage.

1. The Apostles Authored More Than The Canon Contains

The Apostolic Authors illuminate early teaching, the formation of the assemblies of יֵשׁוּעַ/Yeshua and the transmission of the Messiah's message. Together, the authorized Scriptures and the wider memorials reveal the depth and richness of the apostolic heritage. When read alongside the additional acts traditions, they form a unified tapestry of apostolic remembrance that preserves both the teachings and the journeys of those who walked with יֵשׁוּעַ/Yeshua.

These texts invite consideration of the apostles themselves and the way their voices are presented and revealed. Matthew, Peter, and Paul, James the Just (not to be confused with John's brother James), John, and Jude are included in this chapter because they authored the canonical apostolic books, are associated with additional teachings or practices preserved in the early literature of the assemblies of יֵשׁוּעַ/Yeshua, and stand at the intersection of Israel's prophetic memory and the dawning of the Messianic age and the writings held by the early assemblies and followers of יֵשׁוּעַ/Yeshua. James, the brother of יֵשׁוּעַ/Yeshua, was not one of the original twelve disciples yet he penned one of the canonical epistles. This James also wrote two more remarkable books which answer many questions regarding Mary, Joseph and יֵשׁוּעַ/Yeshua's birth, as well as some vital information about John the Baptist and his parents, Elizabeth and Zechariah not included in the Gospel accounts.

Other apostles such as Andrew, Philip, Thomas, Bartholomew, and Barnabas are honored in the early church, yet few writings from their own hands survive. John Mark and Luke, though not among the Twelve, wrote the Gospel accounts that bear their names and carried forward the apostolic witness through their close association with Peter and Paul. The early assemblies preserved not only the voices of the apostles but also the stories of their journeys, teachings, miracles, and martyrdoms, safeguarding every memory connected to those who walked with the Messiah.

2. The Extracanonical Writings Of The Apostles

The extracanonical writings attributed to the apostles and about their ministries, acts, lives and martyrdoms reveal how early believers sought to preserve every memory connected to their lives and teachings. Though not received into the canon, many of these works were treated with deep respect by early assemblies and were remembered for their historical or apostolic associations. Their survival bears witness to the breadth of early devotion within the assemblies of יֵשׁוּעַ/Yeshua and the desire to safeguard every fragment of apostolic tradition.

The Didache: The Teaching of the Twelve Apostles

Among the earliest writings preserved by the assemblies, the *Didache* offers a vivid window into the living memory of the apostolic age. It presents itself as a practical guide for discipleship, worship, and communal life shaped by those who walked with יֵשׁוּעַ/Yeshua. It opens with the ancient moral pattern known as the Two Ways, echoing the teachings of יֵשׁוּעַ/Yeshua and the ethical heritage of Israel. It preserves early apostolic practice with clarity, offering guidance for baptism, fasting, prayer, hospitality, and the breaking of bread, and warning against false apostles and prophets.

Ancient Testimony Referencing the ***Didache***:

> *"The so-called Teachings of the Apostles is used by some." – Eusebius, Ecclesiastical History 3.25.4*

Matthew The Apostle

Matthew's Gospel is the only writing attributed to him, yet early bishops testify that he first wrote it in Hebrew before it was translated into Greek. This detail reveals the Hebrew roots of the apostolic witness before it was widely translated into Greek.

Ancient Testimony Concerning Matthew's Gospel:

> *"Matthew composed the logia in the Hebrew language, and each interpreted them as he was able." – Papias, fragment in Eusebius 3.39.16*
>
> *"Matthew also issued a written Gospel among the Hebrews in their own dialect." – Irenaeus, Against Heresies 3.1.1*

Peter The Apostle

Extracanonical Contributions about Peter include the *Acts of Peter and Paul*, the *Acts of Peter*, the *Apocalypse of Peter*, the *Acts of Peter and Andrew*, and the *Acts of Peter and the Twelve Apostles.*

Ancient Testimony Concerning Extracanonical Writings on Peter:

> *"Let us set before our eyes the good Apostles. Peter, through unjust envy, endured not one or two, but many labors; and thus having borne his testimony, went to his appointed place of glory." – 1 Clement 5:3-4*
>
> *"They relate also the Acts of Peter, in which he contends with Simon." – Irenaeus, Against Heresies 1.23.1*
>
> *"Mark, having become the interpreter of Peter, wrote down accurately whatsoever he remembered." – Eusebius, Ecclesiastical History 3.39.15*
>
> *"In the Acts of Peter it is written that Peter contended with Simon in Rome." – Tertullian, On Baptism 17*

Paul The Apostle

Extracanonical Writings on Paul include *3 Corinthians*, the *Acts of Paul*, the *Acts of Paul and Thecla*, and the *Apocalypse of Paul.*

Ancient Testimony Concerning Extracanonical Writings by or about Paul:

> *"Paul also, having been seven times in bonds, had been driven into exile, had been stoned, had preached in the East and in the West; he taught righteousness to the whole world, having gone to the extremity of the West, and having borne witness before rulers, so he departed from the world and went unto the holy place, having become the greatest example of patient endurance." – 1 Clement 5:5-7*
>
> *"They say that Paul taught abstinence, as the Acts of Paul relate concerning Thecla." – Tertullian, On Baptism 17*

"In the Acts of Paul and Thecla it is written that Paul said, 'Blessed are the pure in heart.'" – Origen, Commentary on Romans 10.31

James the Brother of ‎י‍ֵשׁוּעַ‎/Yeshua

Though James was not one of the twelve, he was the son of Joseph and the brother of ‎יֵשׁוּעַ‎/Yeshua through Joseph's marriage to Mary, and he wrote the canonical epistle that bears his name. Extracanonical Contribution on James includes the *Infancy Gospel of James* (also called *Protoevangelium of James)* about Mary's early life, her betrothal to Joseph, the birth of ‎יֵשׁוּעַ‎/Yeshua and some about his cousin John the Baptist. James also wrote the *History of Joseph the Carpenter*, wherein ‎יֵשׁוּעַ‎/Yeshua recounts to His disciples on the Mount of Olives about the life of Joseph. He was between 80 and 88 years old when he took Mary as his wife. At his death he was one hundred and eleven (111) years old which would have made ‎יֵשׁוּעַ‎/Yeshua 23 to 31 years old when Joseph died. This writing accounts for why Joseph is not mentioned later in ‎יֵשׁוּעַ‎/Yeshua's life, during his ministry or at His crucifixion and why ‎יֵשׁוּעַ‎/Yeshua entrusted Mary to John at Golgatha, saying, "*Behold your mother*" (*John* 19:26–27).

Ancient Testimony Concerning James' Extracanonical Writings:

"There is a book entitled the Birth of Mary, which says that her parents were Joachim and Anna." – Origen, Commentary on Matthew 10.17

"The brethren of Jesus are called sons of Joseph, who had been born to him before Mary." – Origen, Commentary on Matthew 2.17

"They say that the book called the Birth of Mary is read by some…" – Origen, Homilies on Luke 1

"The book called the History of James is read by many of the brethren, for it preserves the memory of the holy family." – Epiphanius, Panarion 78.7

"From the writing, which is called the Birth of Mary, we learn of the parents of the Virgin and the manner of her upbringing." – Jerome, Against Helvidius 7

Jude The Apostle

Extracanonical Writings by or about Jude include the *Epistle of Jude to the Corinthians* and the *Traditions of Jude.*

Ancient Testimony Concerning Extracanonical Writings regarding Jude:

> *"Jude, who wrote the letter, being one of the brothers of the Lord, also left certain traditions which have been preserved by some." – Clement of Alexandria, Hypotyposes (fragment)*
>
> *"Jude wrote a short letter, but one filled with the strong words of heavenly grace, in which he also made use of a prophecy of Enoch." – Origen, Commentary on Matthew 10.17*
>
> *"Jude, in his letter, used testimonies from the book of Enoch, which is not in the canon, yet he employed it for the edification of the faithful." – Didymus the Blind, Commentary on Jude (fragment)*

John The Apostle

The most notable extracanonical writings about John include the *Acts of John* and the *History of John*, works that preserve early traditions about him but whose historical details cannot be verified, though the writings remain of interest.

Ancient Testimony and Historical Facts About John's Later Life:

> *"Irenaeus received this from those who had known John personally, especially Polycarp."Eusebius – Ecclesiastical History 5.20.5–6).*
>
> *"John, the disciple of the Lord, who also had leaned upon His breast, did himself publish a Gospel during his residence at Ephesus in Asia." – Irenaeus, Against Heresies 3.1.1*

Irenaeus appeals to the living memory of the Ephesian church as his source:

> *"Then again, the church in Ephesus, founded by Paul, and having John remaining among them permanently until the times of Trajan, is a true witness of the tradition of the apostles." – Irenaeus, Against Heresies*

3.3.4

Tertullian grounds this in Roman imperial history and apostolic tradition:

"Since, moreover, the Apostle John was banished to the island of Patmos for his testimony to the divine word, we see that the same kind of persecution was continued under Domitian as under Nero." – Tertullian, Prescription Against Heretics 36

Eusebius relies on earlier writers such as Irenaeus and Clement, and on the record of Nerva's edict:

"By Nerva's edict the banished were set free and their confiscated property restored; and it is said that the Apostle John returned from his exile on the island." – Eusebius, Ecclesiastical History 3.20.9 (early 4th century)

Eusebius attributes this to ancient traditions preserved in the churches of Asia:

"After the tyrant's death, John returned from the island of Patmos and took up his abode again at Ephesus." – Eusebius, Ecclesiastical History 3.23.1

Eusebius draws on earlier authorities, especially Irenaeus, and the longstanding Ephesian tradition:

"Tradition relates that the Apostle and Evangelist John survived until the time of Trajan and that he died at Ephesus." – Eusebius, Ecclesiastical History 3.31.3

The Apostolic Acts Literature

The additional acts traditions expand on the ministries of the apostles and offer insight into missionary journeys, miracles, and the spread of the early assemblies. These writings portray the apostles as men taught by יֵשׁוּעַ/Yeshua, shaped by the Spirit, guided by visions, and strengthened by the hope of the coming age. They preserve early memories of courage, suffering, and steadfast proclamation as the good news spread into the wider world.

3. Authentication Of The Apostles' Extracanonical Writings

The ancient testimony surrounding the extracanonical writings of the apostles affirms their early use and preservation within the assemblies' historic and apostolic heritage. The apostles did not write in a vacuum; their voices were guided by the teachings of יֵשׁוּעַ/Yeshua and the treasured Scriptures preserved in the canonical books and extracanonical texts. Early bishops recognized the apostles as the final link in the prophetic chain, quoting the previous prophets, defending their teachings, and preserving their instructions for the generations that followed.

The earliest and most authoritative witnesses include Papias, Irenaeus, Clement of Alexandria, Tertullian, Origen, and Eusebius. These writers preserve firsthand or near-firsthand memory of apostolic teaching, the origins of the Gospels, the ministries of the apostles, and the circulation of early acts traditions. Their testimony forms the historical backbone for understanding how the early assemblies received, preserved, and evaluated the apostolic writings and the acts literature.

4. Edifying Value of the Apostles' Extracanonical Writings for the Modern Reader

The extracanonical writings attributed to the apostles reveal the breadth of early memory within the assemblies ofיֵשׁוּעַ/Yeshua and the reverence with which the first communities preserved every trace of their teaching. The esteem shown to these works by early believers, together with the testimony of ancient authors, demonstrates their contribution to the wider historic witness and enriches the modern reader's understanding of apostolic life and ministry. Read alongside the canonical Scriptures, these memorials illuminate how the earliest followers of יֵשׁוּעַ/Yeshua sought to safeguard every fragment connected to Him. Together, the canonical writings and the wider memorial tradition disclose the depth and enduring richness of the apostolic legacy.

✦✧✦

TWO-FOLD WITNESS:
HOW THE EXTRACANONICAL BOOKS AND ACTS LITERATURE ABOUT THE APOSTLES AFFIRM AND ARE AFFIRMED BY OTHER PROPHETIC WITNESSES

Essential Content From The Other Writings Regarding The Apostles Paralleling The Biblical Authors' Declarations And Teachings:

- *The Didache* preserves early apostolic teaching on ethics, community life, baptism, the breaking of the bread, and the Two Ways (*Acts* 2:42, 46; 20:7; *Luke* 24:35)
- *1 Clement* and the *Epistles of Ignatius* preserve apostolic memory and confirm New Testament traditions.
- *Shepherd of Hermas* reflects early prophetic instruction within the assemblies of יֵשׁוּעַ/Yeshua, paralleling apostolic themes of repentance, purity, and perseverance.
- *The Acts of Paul, Acts of Peter,* and other early apostolic traditions preserve journeys, teachings, and martyrdom accounts not included in canonical *Acts.*
- "Papias… set down in writing the things he had learned from those who had followed the apostles." – Eusebius, *Ecclesiastical History* 3.39.1 (early 4th century)
- "Polycarp, who had been instructed by the apostles, bore witness with steadfastness even unto death." – *Martyrdom of Polycarp* 3.2 (mid-2nd century)
- *The Epistle of Barnabas,* the *Didache*'s companion texts, and the *Epistle to Diognetus* confirm apostolic themes.

New Testament Writings Resonate With Early Apostolic Teachings:

- Matthew 5–7, Acts 2–6, 1 Corinthians 11–14, 1 Peter, 1–3 John, and Revelation 2–3.
- Vision/Ascension of Isaiah and Testaments of the Twelve Patriarchs explicitly reference the Twelve Apostles as prophetic heirs of Israel's long-awaited redemption.

Later Witnesses Reflecting The Long Reception History Of These Writings And The Discernment Of The Assemblies:

- • Origen, Eusebius, Jerome, Epiphanius, Augustine, Clement of Alexandria, Didymus the Blind, and Tertullian
- • The long memory of the apostolic age maintained through bishops, teachers, and ecclesial historians across the centuries

Barnabas

A Son of Encouragement
Preserving Apostolic Instruction

"Barnabas, a servant of the Lord, writes to you concerning the things that make for faith and knowledge." – Teaching of Barnabas 1.1

"And Joses, who by the apostles was surnamed Barnabas, (which is, being interpreted, The son of consolation,) a Levite, and of the country of Cyprus, Having land, sold it, and brought the money, and laid it at the apostles' feet." – Acts 4:36-37

"Barnabas and Paul, men who have risked their lives for the name of our Lord the Messiah." – Acts 15:25-26

"And Barnabas went forth proclaiming the word of life, strengthening the brethren in every place." – Acts of Barnabas 12

"And Barnabas, who was one of the apostles, says: 'Woe to those who are wise for themselves, and prudent in their own sight.'"– Origen, Commentary on John 1.19 (quoting Epistle of Barnabas 4.1)

"Barnabas says, 'We ought therefore, brethren, carefully to inquire concerning our salvation.'" – Clement of Alexandria, Stromata 2.6.31 (quoting Epistle of Barnabas 4.1)

"Barnabas, who was also called Joseph, a Levite born in Cyprus, was ordained an apostle with Paul." – Jerome, De Viris Illustribus 6

Teaching of Barnabas also called Epistle of Barnabas, is associated with the New Testament teacher and apostle Barnabas and rooted in the teachings of יֵשׁוּעַ/Yeshua and in the first-century assemblies, offers insight into covenant interpretation, moral instruction, and the contrast between light and darkness. *Epistle of Barnabas* is not to be confused with the medieval Gnostic fabrication called *Gospel of Barnabas.*

1. Barnabas

> *"Barnabas, who was one of the Seventy disciples, was also a companion of Paul." – Eusebius, Ecclesiastical History 1.12.1*

Barnabas is a significant voice of the early assemblies. Though not one of the original twelve apostles, *Acts* calls him an "apostle," recognizing his authority, faithfulness, and foundational role in the mission to Israel and the nations. A Levite from Cyprus, he served as a bridge between Jerusalem and the wider world, strengthening new communities and guarding the purity of the Gospel (*Acts* 9:27; 11:22–26; 13:2; *1 Corinthians* 9:6).

His writing, known in the ancient church as *Teaching of Barnaba/Epistle of Barnabas (Didaskalia Barnaba)*, reflects a teacher deeply rooted in the covenant and the Scriptures of Israel. Tradition holds that Barnabas preached in Cyprus and was martyred there (*Acts of Barnabas* authored by John Mark, also the author of the *Gospel of Mark*), demonstrating Barnabas' faithfulness to the end.

2. *Teaching of Barnabas* Also Called *Epistle of Barnabas*

Teaching of Barnaba/Epistle of Barnabas interprets the Torah and the Prophets as pointing to יְשׁוּעַ/Yeshua the Messiah and the renewal of the covenant. It draws deeply from *Genesis, Exodus, Leviticus, Deuteronomy,* the *Psalms, Isaiah, Jeremiah,* and *Daniel,* as well as early writings such as *1 Enoch, Jubilees, Testaments of the Twelve Patriarchs,* and the *Didache.* Scripture forms the structure through which Barnabas explains the New Covenant of the Messiah, and the life of the assemblies.

A central feature is the teaching on The Two Ways – the Way of Life and the Way of Death – also found in *Deuteronomy 30, Psalm 1*, *Proverbs,* the *Didache*, and the *Testaments of the Twelve Patriarchs.* The Way of Life is marked by humility, righteousness, generosity, purity, and love of neighbor, the Way of Death by idolatry, greed, violence, deceit, and lawlessness. This ethical framework shaped early discipleship.

Barnabas interprets the commandments as prophetic symbols pointing to יֵשׁוּעַ/Yeshua and the renewed covenant. Circumcision points to the heart. Dietary laws teach moral discernment. The Sabbath is fulfilled in the Messiah. Sacrifices foreshadow His self-offering. Through this approach, the earliest believers understood themselves not as abandoning the Scriptures of Israel but entering into their fullness.

3. Authentication Of *The Epistle/Teaching of Barnabas*

The *Teaching of Barnabas/Epistle of Barnabas* is preserved in the Codex Sinaiticus, the fourth-century codex (collection) of Greek manuscripts found at St. Catherine's Monastery located near a mountain named Sinai, Egypt called Jebel Musa, traditionally associated with Sinai, but not the same as the Biblical Mount Sinai. Codex Sinaiticus also contains the *Shepherd of Hermas* along with the canonized New Testament books. The inclusion of *Teaching of Barnaba/Epistle of Barnabas* in this codex shows that some early assemblies valued these writings and circulated them alongside apostolic books.

Against this backdrop, Eusebius' comments take on added significance, as he records that some writings were widely recognized despite ongoing debate within the early assemblies:

> *"Among the disputed books, which are nevertheless recognized by many, is the so-called Epistle of Barnabas." and that "The Shepherd of Hermas is likewise reckoned among the disputed books." – Eusebius, Ecclesiastical History 3.25.4*

Early Christian writers also discussed the authorship of *Hebrews*, and many regarded Barnabas as a plausible author due to his Levitical background and theological depth.

> *"For there is extant withal an Epistle to the Hebrews under the name of Barnabas." – Tertullian, On Modesty 20*

> *"Some say that the Epistle to the Hebrews is by Barnabas." – Clement of*

Alexandria quoted by Eusebius, Ecclesiastical History 6.14.2

"Some have ascribed the Epistle to the Hebrews to Clement… others to Luke… others to Barnabas." – Eusebius, Ecclesiastical History 3.38.2

These testimonies show that Barnabas' voice was respected, his teaching widely known, and his authority recognized among early assemblies.

4. Edifying Value of *The Epistle/Teaching of Barnabas* for the Modern Reader

Epistle/Teaching of Barnabas offers a window into how the earliest assemblies interpreted the Scriptures of Israel in light of the Messiah. It preserves the memory of a teacher who saw the Torah not as abolished but fulfilled, its symbols pointing to the inward transformation promised by the prophets.

Barnabas' ethical instruction – especially the Two Ways tradition – directed early apostolic discipleship and provided a moral framework for communities desiring to walk in the light of the Messiah. For Barnabas, the commandments were prophetic symbols pointing to the Messiah, the new heart, and the renewed covenant.

For modern readers, *Epistle/Teaching of Barnabas* reveals how the earliest believers understood their identity as a covenant people, how they read the Scriptures of Israel, and how they embraced the Messiah as the culmination of the Law and the Prophets. It invites readers to recover early interpretation, to see the unity of the covenants, and to walk in the Way of Life that Barnabas so clearly described.

———— ✦✧✦ ————

TWO-FOLD WITNESS:
HOW EPISTLE/TEACHINGS OF BARNABAS AFFIRM AND ARE AFFIRMED BY OTHER PROPHETIC WITNESSES

Essential Content From Epistle/Teachings Of Barnabas Paralleling Biblical Author's Declarations And Teachings:

- Typology and covenantal symbolism parallel the interpretive methods used in *Hebrews*, especially the spiritual meaning of sacrifices, circumcision, priesthood, and covenant signs. Barnabas' reading of Torah through Messiah's fulfillment resonates with *Hebrews* 8–10 and *Romans* 2:28-29.
- The "Two Ways" teaching is shared with the *Didache* and the *Testaments of the Twelve Patriarchs*, revealing a widespread early tradition of ethical formation rooted in *Deuteronomy* 30, *Psalm* 1, and the wisdom literature. This framework shaped the earliest assemblies' understanding of covenantal faithfulness, community life, and moral discernment.
- The spiritual meaning of Torah resonates with Paul's and the author of *Hebrews*' frameworks. Barnabas' emphasis on the inward covenant, the circumcision of the heart, and the prophetic reading of Scripture parallels *Romans* 2, *Galatians* 3–4, and *Hebrews* 4–10.

Additional Ancient Writings Supporting Barnabas' Themes:

- The *Didache* (ethical and covenantal parallels, shared Two Ways tradition, early community instruction)
- *Testaments of the Twelve Patriarchs* (shared moral framework, messianic expectation, covenantal ethics)
- *Jubilees* (covenantal symbolism, sacred time, angelic mediation)
- *1 Enoch* (judgment, righteousness, heavenly books, prophetic
- interpretation)
- *Ecclesiasticus/Sirach* (wisdom, ethical formation, covenant memory)
- *Wisdom of Solomon* (righteousness, divine justice, eschatological hope)

New Testament Writings Resonating With Barnabas' Themes:

- *Matthew* 5–7 (ethical instruction, covenant fulfillment, Two Ways imagery)

- *Romans* 2–4 (circumcision of the heart, covenant identity, covenant faithfulness)
- *Galatians* 3–4 (allegory, covenant interpretation, Torah and promise)
- *Hebrews* 8–10 (new covenant, priesthood, sacrificial symbolism)
- *James* 1–3 (ethical formation, moral testing, righteousness)
- *Revelation* 2–3 (ethical exhortation, perseverance, covenant faithfulness)

✦✧✦

Gospel Of Nicodemus/ Acts Of Pilate

An Early Witness to the Trial, Crucifixion, Descent, and Resurrection of the Messiah

"You will not abandon my soul to the realm of the dead, nor will You allow Your Holy One to see decay." – Psalm 16:10

"You will not abandon my soul to Hades, nor let your Holy One see corruption." – Acts 2:27 (a Greek quote of Hebrew Psalm 16:10)

"For just as Jonah was three days and three nights in the belly of the great fish, so will the Son of Man be three days and three nights in the heart of the earth." – Spoke by יֵשׁוּעַ/Yeshua in Matthew 12:40

"And the King of Glory entered, and the eternal gates were broken before Him." – Gospel of Nicodemus/Acts of Pilate

The Acts of Pilate and Gospel of Nicodemus, rooted in early passion traditions and attributed to compilers within the first-century assemblies, offering insight into the trial, death, and descent narratives surrounding the Messiah.

1. Authors

The *Gospel of Nicodemus/Acts of Pilate* attributes its testimony to figures known from the canonical Gospels. These attributions arise from the devotional memory of the early assemblies, who sought to preserve the accounts of those closest to the Messiah's passion. The text presents the voices of Pontius Pilate, Nicodemus, Joseph of Arimathea, Annas,

Caiaphas, and the two resurrected witnesses Leucius and Charinus.

The structure of the work suggests that its compiler drew upon earlier traditions, legal-style narratives, and liturgical retellings. The trial scenes resemble judicial transcripts, while the descent narrative reflects homiletic and prophetic traditions shared among early assemblies. The author or compiler remains anonymous, yet the work bears the marks of someone deeply familiar with the Gospel accounts, early preaching, and Jewish apocalyptic expectation.

The text came to be linked with Nicodemus because its narrative unfolds through the testimony of figures who appear in the Gospel accounts, especially those – like Nicodemus – who defended Jesus and witnessed His burial. At the same time, because the text presents itself as a detailed record of the judicial proceedings before Pontius Pilate, its content naturally led to the designation *Acts of Pilate*, reflecting its focus on Pilate's role and the courtroom events surrounding the crucifixion.

2. The *Gospel of Nicodemus/Acts of Pilate*

The *Gospel of Nicodemus/Acts of Pilate* preserves early passion traditions surrounding the trial, death, descent, and resurrection of יֵשׁוּעַ/Yeshua. Its first section presents a legal and historical witness to the trial before Pilate, including Nicodemus' defense of יֵשׁוּעַ/Yeshua, Joseph of Arimathea's request for the body, Pilate's reluctance to condemn Him, testimony of the healed, confession of the Roman soldiers, and the political pressure of the Sanhedrin. These scenes echo the Gospel accounts while expanding the dramatic tension surrounding the trial.

The second section records the testimony of the resurrected saints, recalling *Matthew* 27:52–53. The resurrected brothers Leucius and Charinus recount what they witnessed in Hades, the moment יֵשׁוּעַ/Yeshua broke the gates, the liberation of the righteous souls who were waiting there, the defeat of death, the restoration of Adam to Paradise, and the fulfillment of ancient prophecy.

The Harrowing of Hell narrative portrays the mystery of the three days that יֵשׁוּעַ/Yeshua was in the tomb. The text describes the terror of Satan, the authority of יֵשׁוּעַ/Yeshua, the joy of the patriarchs, the fulfillment of prophecy, and the restoration of humanity. Adam, Eve, Seth, Enoch, Abraham, Isaac, Jacob, Isaiah, David, Solomon, the prophets, John the Baptist, and the repentant thief recognize Him as the One they foretold. The Messiah fulfills the promise that He would "lead captivity captive" (*Psalm* 68:18; *Ephesians* 4:8), proclaim victory to "the spirits in prison" (*1 Peter* 3:18–19), triumph over the powers of darkness (*Colossians* 2:15), and take "the keys of death and of Hades" (*Revelation* 1:18).

The text also expands the "Sign of Jonah" (*Matthew* 12:40; 16:4; *Luke* 11:29–30), presenting Jonah's descent as the prophetic pattern fulfilled in the Messiah's true descent and triumph.

Enoch's words from Paradise concerning his and Elijah's return in the last days align with *Apocalypse of Elijah, Zechariah 4, History of Joseph the Carpenter*, and *Revelation* 11, identifying the two prophets – the two witnesses, the two olive trees that "stand before the Lord of the whole earth," and the two lampstands (plural of מנורה – menorah) – as Enoch and Elijah, a particularly valuable connection for modern readers interested in eschatological prophecy.

3. Authentication Of *Gospel Of Nicodemus/Acts Of Pilate*

Gospel of Nicodemus/Acts of Pilate stands as one of the most vivid extracanonical accounts of the death, descent, and resurrection of יֵשׁוּעַ/Yeshua. Though not part of the canon, it preserves early testimony to His victory over death and the mystery of the "Sign of Jonah."

The text illustrates the difference between (a) internal claims and (b) scholarly dating:

(a) Internal Claim (Self-Attestation):

> "The things which Nicodemus wrote in Hebrew and left behind are preserved by those who have received them." – *Gospel of Nicodemus, Prologue.*

External References:

> *"The Acts of Pilate were made known to the emperor, containing everything concerning Christ." – Justin Martyr, First Apology 35*

> *"And that these things were so, you may learn from the Acts of Pontius Pilate." – Justin Martyr, First Apology 48*

> *"The Acts of Pilate, which were composed at that time, show that these things happened." – Tertullian, Apology 21*

These references show that *Gospel of Nicodemus/Acts of Pilate* circulated widely and was used by early believers as a witness to the Messiah's innocence and the truth of His passion, His resurrection and the resurrection of many who formerly had died.

> *"And the graves were opened; and many bodies of the saints which slept arose, And came out of the graves after his resurrection, and went into the holy city, and appeared unto many." – Matthew 27:52–53*

(b) Scholarly Dating and the Age of Manuscripts

While the internal claims of *Gospel of Nicodemus/Acts of Pilate* reflect the time when the events occurred and when the accounts were first recorded, while scholarly dating of the text (AD 150–250) reflects the age of the surviving manuscripts and the results of literary analysis. These two categories are not the same. The events themselves belong to the first century, during and shortly after the crucifixion and resurrection, while the written forms that survive today represent later copies.

Confusing these categories leads to unnecessary doubt, a difficulty that has affected many early accounts from those who lived during the lifetime of יֵשׁוּעַ/Yeshua and the apostles.

The preservation of the *Gospel of Nicodemus/Acts of Pilate* in multiple languages and manuscript traditions indicates that early believers valued it as a witness to the innocence of the Messiah, the justice of יהוה/*Yahweh*, and the unseen triumph that unfolded between the cross and the resurrection.

4. Edifying Value of *Gospel of Nicodemus/Acts of Pilate* for the Modern Reader

Seen through this lens, *Gospel of Nicodemus/Acts of Pilate* reveals its enduring prophetic value and its contribution to the wider Scriptural witness. The text presents יֵשׁוּעַ/Yeshua's death as conquering victory, His descent as triumphant, and His resurrection as public and cosmic in scope. His victory extends to the dead, the living, and the ages to come.

The expanded trial scenes highlight the contrast between human injustice and divine righteousness, recalling Isaiah's suffering servant (*Isaiah* 52:13–53:12) and the Psalm of the innocent sufferer (*Psalm* 22). The descent narrative resonates with prophetic images of gates lifted up and captives set free. Through these scenes, the text declares that the Messiah's humiliation leads to exaltation, and that His judgment is both terrible and merciful.

The *Gospel of Nicodemus/Acts of Pilate* reinforces key truths already proclaimed in the canonical Gospels: יֵשׁוּעַ/Yeshua's innocence, His true death, His descent, His resurrection, and His fulfillment of prophecy. By giving voice to Nicodemus, Joseph of Arimathea, the Roman guards, and the resurrected saints, the text amplifies the chorus of witnesses who confess Him as the Righteous One.

For modern readers, the *Gospel of Nicodemus/Acts of Pilate* offers a vivid portrayal of the Messiah's triumph over death, the liberation of the righteous, and the cosmic scope of redemption. It invites believers to stand in awe before the King who judges justly, descends in mercy, and rises in glory.

———— ✦✧✦ ————

TWO-FOLD WITNESS:
HOW *GOSPEL OF NICODEMUS/ACTS OF PILATE* AFFIRMS AND IS AFFIRMED BY OTHER PROPHETIC WITNESSES

Essential Content From *Acts Of Pilate/Gospel Of Nicodemus* Clarifying The Biblical Authors' Declarations And Teachings:

- *Gospel of Nicodemus/Acts of Pilate* preserves early traditions about the trial, crucifixion, and resurrection of יֵשׁוּעַ/Yeshua, illuminating how the early church remembered these events. Its courtroom scenes, testimonies, and narrative details echo the passion accounts in *Matthew 26–28*, *Luke 22–24*, and *John* 18–21, revealing how the earliest believers defended the innocence of the Messiah and the injustice of His condemnation.
- The descent into Hades narrative known as "*The Harrowing of Hell*" clarifies the understanding preserved in the earliest assemblies of יֵשׁוּעַ/Yeshua's victory over death and the unseen realm. This vivid portrayal of the Messiah breaking the gates of Sheol, liberating the righteous, and overthrowing the powers of darkness parallels *1 Peter* 3:18-20, *Ephesians* 4:8-10, and the resurrection imagery of *Revelation* 1:17-18.
- The testimonies of witnesses in the text reflect early apologetic efforts to defend the truth of the resurrection. The accounts of Nicodemus, Joseph of Arimathea, the centurion, and the resurrected saints mirror the apologetic tone of *Acts* 2–4, *1 Corinthians* 15, and *Matthew* 27:52-53, demonstrating how the early assemblies articulated the historical reality of the risen Messiah.
- The narrative parallels themes in *1 Peter* 3–4 regarding proclamation to the spirits in prison. The descent scenes echo Peter's teaching on the Messiah's proclamation to the imprisoned spirits, the vindication of the righteous, and the triumph of divine justice over the powers of the unseen world.

Ancient Writings Supporting *Gospel of Nicodemus/Acts of Pilate's* Themes:

- Apostolic Fathers (early resurrection preaching, witness under persecution, and the continuity of apostolic proclamation; parallels with *1 Clement, Epistles of Ignatius,* and *Epistle of Polycarp to the Philippians*)

- *1 Enoch* and *2 Esdras* (imagery of the underworld, divine judgment, resurrection hope, and the vindication of the righteous; parallels with *Daniel* 7–12 and *Revelation* 20–22)
- *Testaments of the Twelve Patriarchs* (messianic deliverance, judgment, resurrection hope)
- *Apocryphon of Abraham* (heavenly ascent, judgment of nations, cosmic conflict)
- *Jubilees* (angelic mediation, covenantal justice, sacred time)
- *2 Baruch* and *4 Ezra* (lament over Jerusalem, resurrection, divine justice)
- *Shepherd of Hermas* (angelic oversight, repentance, divine discipline)

New Testament Writings Confirming Themes Within *The Acts Of Pilate/Gospel of Nicodemus*:

- *Matthew* 27–28 (trial, crucifixion, resurrection, earthquake, resurrected saints)
- *Luke* 23–24 (innocence of the Messiah, testimony of witnesses, resurrection)
- *John* 18–21 (trial scenes, eyewitness testimony, vindication)
- *Acts* 2–4 (apostolic proclamation of the resurrection, defense before authorities)
- *Romans* 5–6 (death defeated, new life through the Messiah)
- *1 Corinthians* 15 (resurrection, victory over death, eyewitness testimony)
- *Ephesians* 4:8-10 (descent and ascent of the Messiah)
- *1 Peter* 3–4 (proclamation to the spirits, suffering, vindication)
- Revelation 1, 5, 20–22 (keys of death and Hades, judgment, new creation)

SIXTH ERA:
The Early Bishops

Clement or Rome

The Peacemaker Who Preserved Apostolic Order and Unity

"Thus saith the Lord, Stand ye in the ways, and see, and ask for the old paths, where is the good way, and walk therein, and ye shall find rest for your souls." – Jeremiah 6:16

"Remember them which have the rule over you, who have spoken unto you the word of God (יהוה/Yahweh): whose faith follow, considering the end of their conversation." – Hebrews 13:7

"And I intreat thee also, true yokefellow, help those women which laboured with me in the gospel, with Clement also, and with other my fellowlabourers, whose names are in the Book of Life." – Philippians 4:3

"Let us fix our eyes on the blood of Christ and understand how precious it is to His Father." – 1 Clement 7:4

The writing attributed to Clement of Rome situated within the late first and early second centuries, offers insight into early order within the assemblies, humility, and the preservation of apostolic teaching. Clement of Rome is not to be confused with Clement of Alexandria as these two were entirely different figures, separated by more than a century and writing in different regions and contexts.

1. Clement of Rome as an Author

Clement of Rome, writing in the late 1st century, stands as one of the earliest and most trusted voices of the post-apostolic age. Ancient testimony consistently presents Clement as a man walking with the apostles and entrusted with their teaching:

> *"Clement also, who was appointed third bishop of the Church at Rome, was a man of great reputation and of approved character." – Eusebius, Ecclesiastical History 3.15.1 (early 4th century)*
>
> *"Clement, of whom the apostle Paul makes mention, was the fourth bishop of Rome after Peter." – Jerome, Lives of Illustrious Men 15 (late 4th century)*
>
> *"Clement, who had conversed with the apostles, preserved their teaching with exactness and handed it down to the churches." – Epiphanius, Panarion 27.6.1 (late 4th century)*
>
> *"Clement, a man of apostolic times, was renowned for the purity of his life and the firmness of his faith." – Rufinus, Ecclesiastical History 3.34 (early 5th century)*

Appointed as a leading elder of the assembly at Rome, Clement was mentored by Peter and Paul and served as a stabilizing shepherd in the earliest post-apostolic generation. Irenaeus records the succession:

> *"The blessed apostles, then, having founded and built up the Church, committed into the hands of Linus the office of the episcopate. Of this Linus Paul makes mention in the Epistles to Timothy. To him succeeded Anacletus, and after him, in the third place from the apostles, Clement was allotted the bishopric." – Irenaeus, Against Heresies 3.3.3*

2. Clement's Writings

Clement's surviving work, *1 Clement*, addresses a crisis in the Corinthian assembly – one Paul had confronted repeatedly. The letter calls the believers back to humility, unity, and obedience, grounding its exhortations in the Scriptures of Israel and the example of the apostles.

Clement appeals to the order established by Peter, Paul, and the early overseers, reminding the Corinthians that the apostles appointed leaders with the consent of the assemblies. His writing reflects the pastoral heart of the first-century church: urging repentance, restoring peace, and reestablishing the order disrupted by jealousy and factionalism.

Throughout the letter, Clement draws on Moses, Isaiah, the Psalms, and the prophets, interpreting their witness in light of the Messiah and applying it to the life of the assemblies. His exhortations echo the prophetic summons to justice, humility, and covenant faithfulness, showing how the earliest believers understood themselves as the continuation of Israel's story.

3. Authentication of Clement's Writings

The ancient testimony surrounding Clement's writing affirms the authenticity of *1 Clement* and reveals how it was preserved and relied upon within the early assemblies.

> *"Clement also… was a man of great reputation and of approved character." – Eusebius, Ecclesiastical History 3.15.1*
>
> *"In the twelfth year of Domitian, Clement succeeded Anencletus in the bishopric of the Church of Rome." – Eusebius, Ecclesiastical History 3.34.1*
>
> *"Clement, of whom the apostle Paul makes mention…" – Jerome, Lives of Illustrious Men 15*
>
> *"Clement… preserved their teaching with exactness." – Epiphanius, Panarion 27.6.1*

1 Clement was widely read in the early assemblies and considered by some to be on par with the apostolic writings. It appears in several manuscript collections treasured by communities planted by the apostles and was used for instruction, encouragement, and correction. Its circulation across the Mediterranean world shows the trust placed in Clement as a guardian of unity and righteousness. To read *1 Clement* is to hear apostolic teaching before the dust of the 1st century had settled. His letter stands as one of the earliest and clearest witnesses to the continuity of apostolic doctrine in the generation immediately following the apostles.

Clement also appears as an important character in the *Shepherd of Hermas*, where Hermas is instructed to deliver his message – the book of *Shepherd of Hermas* – to Clement for distribution to the assemblies abroad:

"Clement will send it to the cities abroad, for this is his duty." – Shepherd of Hermas, Vision 2.4.

This internal evidence confirms that Hermas and Clement were active in Rome at the same time and that Clement exercised recognized authority in sending writings to other assemblies. From the martyrdoms of Peter in AD 64 and Paul in AD 67 to Clement's leadership in the final decade of the first century and the ministry of Hermas within that same generation, the early Roman assembly reflects a continuous line of witnesses. This coherence also explains why later tradition remembered and recorded Hermas as the older brother of Pius, whose episcopate did not begin until the mid-second century, allowing both the kinship tradition and the early dating of Hermas' work to stand without contradiction.

4. Edifying Value for the Modern Reader

Seen through this lens, *1 Clement* reveals its enduring apostolic value and its contribution to the wider Scriptural witness. It offers one of the clearest windows into the pastoral heart of the first-century assemblies – calling believers to humility, obedience, repentance, and unity.

Clement's voice stands firmly in the prophetic stream that summons the people of יֵשׁוּעַ/Yeshua to righteousness and covenant faithfulness. His letter demonstrates how the earliest believers interpreted the Scriptures of Israel in light of the Messiah and applied them to real crises within their communities.

For modern readers, Clement's writing offers more than historical insight. It reveals the heartbeat of the early assemblies: steadfast devotion to Scriptural truth, unity grounded in humility, and a commitment to the order established by the apostles. It reminds believers that the path of righteousness is marked by service, peace, and faithfulness to the revelation entrusted to the assemblies of יֵשׁוּעַ/Yeshua.

TWO-FOLD WITNESS: HOW CLEMENT'S WRITINGS AFFIRM AND ARE AFFIRMED BY OTHER PROPHETIC WITNESSES

Essential Content From Clement's Writing Clarifying The Biblical Authors' Declarations And Teachings:

- *1 Clement* preserves early apostolic teaching on unity, humility, and church order, illuminating themes found in Paul's Corinthian correspondence. Clement's exhortations mirror *1 Corinthians* 1-4,
- *Philippians* 2, and *Hebrews* 13, revealing how the earliest post-apostolic generation understood leadership, harmony, and the dangers of factionalism.
- Clement's use of Scripture and early traditions clarifies how the first post-apostolic generation interpreted the Hebrew Bible. His citations of *Genesis, Isaiah, Psalm*, and *Job* demonstrate a continuity of prophetic interpretation that aligns with hermeneutics of *Hebrews, Romans,* and *1 Peter.*
- Clement's emphasis on righteousness, repentance, and divine order parallels the ethical frameworks of the *Testaments of the Twelve Patriarchs.*
- Clement's moral exhortations echo the covenantal ethics of *Testament of Judah, Testament of Levi*, and the Two Ways tradition found in the *Didache* and *Epistle of Barnabas.*
- □Clement's references to the phoenix and other symbols demonstrate how the followers of יֵשׁוּעַ/Yeshua engaged early with creation motifs and divine renewal. These symbolic illustrations parallel the resurrection imagery of *1 Corinthians* 15, the new-creation themes of *Isaiah* 65–66, and the cosmic renewal of *Revelation* 21–22.

Additional Ancient Writings Supporting Clementine Themes:

- *Shepherd of Hermas* (shared themes of repentance, divine discipline, angelic oversight, and the moral formation of the early assemblies)
- Josephus and Philo (context for leadership, virtue, communal order, and the moral expectations placed upon the righteous)
- The *Didache* (Two Ways tradition, community order, ethical instruction)

- *Testaments of the Twelve Patriarchs* (ethical exhortation, covenantal faithfulness and righteousness, messianic expectation)
- *1 Enoch* (divine judgment, righteousness, heavenly order)
- *Jubilees* (covenantal obedience, sacred time, angelic mediation)
- *1 Baruch* and *2 Baruch* (repentance, divine justice, restoration)

New Testament Writings Resonating With *Clement's* Pastoral And Ethical Themes:

- *Matthew* 5–7 (ethical formation, humility, righteousness)
- *John* 13–17 (unity, love, obedience)
- *Acts* 20 (shepherding, leadership integrity, guarding the flock)
- *Romans* 12–15 (communal harmony, humility, moral transformation)
- *1 Corinthians* 1–4 and 12–14 (unity, order, spiritual maturity)
- *Philippians* 2 (humility, imitation of Christ)
- *Hebrews* 12–13 (discipline, perseverance, leadership)
- *James* 1–3 (righteousness, speech, moral integrity)

✦✧✦

Shepherd Of Hermas

A Prophetic Call to Repentance, Purity, and Faithfulness

A direct quotation from the Shepherd of Hermas, Mandate 1.1. by Irenaeus: "Well did the Scripture speak, saying, 'First of all, believe that God is one, who created and completed all things.'"
– Irenaeus, Against Heresies 4.20.2

"Wherefore also in the Shepherd it is written, 'First of all believe that God is one.'" – Clement of Alexandria, Stromata 1.29.181

"I think that the book of the Shepherd is divinely inspired."
– Origen, Commentary on Romans 10.31

"If then ye prepare yourselves, and repent with all your heart, and turn to the Lord, it will be possible for you to escape it, if your heart be pure and spotless, and ye spend the rest of the days of your life in serving the Lord blamelessly. Cast your cares upon the Lord, and He will direct them. Trust the Lord, ye who doubt, for He is all-powerful, and can turn His anger away from you, and send scourges" on the doubters. Woe to those who hear these words and despise them: better were it for them not to have been born."
– Shepherd of Hermas, Vision 4.2

***Shepherd of Hermas*, a widely read early text** circulating among the followers of יֵשׁוּעַ/Yeshua and situated within the early Roman assemblies, offers insight into repentance, moral renewal, and the shaping of a faithful community.

1. Author

The text invites us to consider the writer Hermas himself and the way his voice is presented and revealed. Several writers from the early centuries after the apostolic era speak of Hermas.

"Hermas, who wrote the book called The Shepherd, is said to have been the brother of Pius, bishop of Rome." – Origen, Homilies on Luke 1 (early 3rd century)

"Hermas, the author of the book called The Shepherd, is said to have been the brother of Pius, who was bishop of Rome." – Eusebius, Ecclesiastical History 3.3.6 (312–325)

"Hermas, the author of the book called the Shepherd, is said to have been the brother of Pius, bishop of Rome." – Jerome, Lives of Illustrious Men 10 (late 4th century)

"But Hermas wrote the Shepherd very recently, in our times, in the city of Rome, while his brother Pius sat in the chair of the church of Rome." – Muratorian Fragment 74–77(170–200 AD)

Hermas' Connection to Clement

Shepherd of Hermas itself records that Hermas was instructed to place his writings in the hands of Clement (*Shepherd of Hermas, Vision 2.4*) so they could be sent to the other assemblies, a detail that presupposes both men were alive and serving in Rome at the same time. This places Hermas within the same late first century circle of leadership as Clement and shows that his work was valued enough to be copied and circulated broadly. From the martyrdoms of Peter and Paul during Nero's reign, through the leadership of Clement in the final decade of the first century, to the ministry of Hermas in that same generation and the later episcopate of his younger brother Pius in AD 140–154, the succession of witnesses forms a coherent and continuous line within the Roman assembly. A more coherent explanation for the later chronological tension is that Hermas was the older brother of Pius, writing *The Shepherd* during Clement's lifetime in the final decades of the first century, while Pius, being significantly younger, did not become bishop until the mid-second century. This allows the internal evidence, the kinship tradition preserved by Eusebius, and the early circulation of Hermas' writings to stand together without contradiction.

2. *Shepherd of Hermas* and Its Contents

Shepherd of Hermas is one of the most remarkable and influential writings that the early assemblies revered. The writing bears the original Greek title *Ποιμὴν Ἑρμᾶ (Poimēn Hermā)* translated as *Shepherd of Hermas*. Composed in Rome in the late 1st century (owing to Hermas' relationship with Clement and Paul). Hermas presents his work as a series of visions, commandments/mandates, and parables delivered by heavenly messengers – most notably a "Shepherd" who serves as his guide, and in one place calls Himself "the angel of repentance." (*Shepherd of Hermas, Mandate* 6.2).

Visions:

Hermas receives symbolic visions revealing the need for repentance. The most famous is the vision of the tower built from living stones, representing the people of י_שוע_/Yeshua (*1 Corinthians* 3:9-17).

Commandments/Mandates:

These moral teachings, delivered by the angelic shepherd, emphasize purity, truthfulness, patience, humility, forgiveness, resisting the devil, and trusting in י_שוע_/Yeshua (*James* 4:7-10). The mandates form an early manual of apostolic discipleship among the followers of י_שוע_/Yeshua, calling believers to live lives worthy of their confession.

Similitudes or Parables:

These parables use vivid imagery – trees, mountains, servants, vineyards – to teach about judgment, mercy, and the consequences of sin (*Matthew* 13:1-23). They reinforce the central message of the book: repentance remains possible, but it must be sincere and accompanied by transformation.

His visions portray the assembly as a tower built from living stones, revealing י_שוע_/Yeshua's ongoing work to prepare a holy people (*1 Peter* 2:4-5). Stones that are cracked or broken are set aside until restored through repentance, echoing Ezekiel's promise of renewal and

Zechariah's vision of a purified people (*Ezekiel* 36:25-27; *Zechariah* 3:1-5).

> *"The Son of God is the foundation, and the whole building is supported by Him." – Shepherd of Hermas, Similitude 9.14*

The central theme of the *Shepherd of Hermas* is "repentance". The book insists that יֵשׁוּעַ/Yeshua, in His mercy, grants believers the opportunity to turn back to Him if they have committed iniquity even after baptism (*Acts* 3:19;8:22; *1 John* 1:9; *Revelation* 2:5; *Ezekiel* 18:21–23; *Joel* 2:12–13; *Didache* 4.14; *2 Clement* 8.2–4; *Epistle/Teaching of Barnabas* 19.12 *Shepherd of Hermas, Mandate* 4.1–4.4; *Mandate* 12.1–6; *Similitude* 5.6–7). This teaching was deeply influential in the early church, which struggled with how to respond to sin, especially during persecution. Hermas' message is both stern and hopeful: stern because sin has real consequences, hopeful because יֵשׁוּעַ/Yeshua, the Son of יהוה/*Yahweh*'s mercy is greater than human failure (*Psalm* 103:8-12). Through the *Shepherd of Hermas*, the early assemblies learned that repentance is the doorway to renewal, that holiness is the fruit of obedience, and that the mercy of יהוה/*Yahweh* remains the anchor of every generation that seeks Him with a sincere heart.

3. Authentication

The ancient testimony surrounding *Shepherd of Hermas* provides evidence of its authenticity and reveals how it was preserved within the early assemblies' apostolic heritage. A considerable number of early church fathers and writers noted the existence of the *Shepherd of Hermas.* Since these men carry much historical stature in the early assemblies, *Shepherd of Hermas* should not have been left out of the later canonical collection.

> *"Wherefore also in the Shepherd it is written, 'First of all believe that God is one…'" – Clement of Alexandria, Stromata 1.29.181*
>
> *"Well did the Scripture speak, saying, 'First of all believe that God is one…'" – Irenaeus, Against Heresies 4.20.2 (This line is a direct quotation from*

Shepherd of Hermas, Mandate 1.)

"I think that the book of the Shepherd is divinely inspired." – Origen, Commentary on Romans 10.31

"I would admit your argument, if the writing of the Shepherd deserved to be included in the Divine Instrument; but every council of the churches has judged it apocryphal." – Tertullian, On Modesty 10

"There are also other books, not included in the canon, but appointed by the Fathers to be read by those who newly join us… such as the Shepherd." – Athanasius, Festal Letter 39

4. Edifying Value of *Shepherd of Hermas* for the Modern Reader

Shepherd of Hermas provides an exhaustive teaching regarding a believer's conduct in the same fashion as the apostles. It can prompt the reader to reconsider the fear and awe of יהוה/*Yahweh* triggering a serious response leading to repentance from sin and a swift return to righteousness. *The Shepherd of Hermas* portrays that repentance is not a single moment but a lifelong posture (*Ezekiel* 18:30-32; *Hosea* 14:1-2). Hermas' *Shepherd* reminds every generation that יהוה/Yahweh's mercy is greater than human failure, yet repentance must be sincere and accompanied by transformation (*Romans* 12:1-2). Hermas preserves the apostolic witness by calling believers to embody the fundamental teachings they had received from the apostles.

This balance of sternness and hope made the book a treasured companion for believers seeking assurance that restoration was possible. Through Hermas, the vine of righteousness was nurtured with mercy, strengthened with discipline, and prepared to bear fruit in the generations to come (*John* 15:1-8).

✦✧✦

TWO-FOLD WITNESS:
HOW THE *SHEPHERD OF HERMAS* AFFIRMS AND IS AFFIRMED BY OTHER PROPHETIC WITNESSES

Essential Content From The *Shepherd Of Hermas* Clarifying The Biblical Authors' Declarations And Teachings:

- *Shepherd of Hermas* preserves early teaching handed down among the followers of יֵשׁוּעַ/Yeshua and the apostles on repentance, restoration, and moral transformation. Its call to return to יהוה/*Yahweh* with sincerity echoes the prophetic summons of *Ezekiel* 18:30-32 and *Hosea* 14:1-2, clarifying how the earliest assemblies understood repentance as a lifelong posture rather than a single moment.
- The vision of the tower built from living stones illuminates the apostolic imagery of the people of יהוה/*Yahweh* as a spiritual house (*1 Peter* 2:4-5). Hermas' depiction of stones being assessed, evaluated, tested, purified, or set aside until restored parallels Paul's teaching on the testing of each believer's work (*1 Corinthians* 3:9-17).
- The mandates reinforce the apostolic moral vision found in James, Peter, and Paul. Hermas' emphasis on purity, humility, patience, forgiveness, and resisting the devil aligns with *James* 1:21-27; *1 Peter* 1:13-16; and *Galatians* 5:22-23, clarifying how early believers applied these teachings in daily life.
- The parables (similitudes) illustrate the consequences of sin and the hope of restoration, echoing the Messiah's own parables in *Matthew* 13 and *Luke* 15. Hermas' insistence that repentance remains possible "even after baptism" clarifies early debates among the followers of יֵשׁוּעַ/Yeshua and the apostles, as reflected in *Hebrews* 6:1-6; 12:5-11.
- The Shepherd's warnings against double-mindedness, hypocrisy, and spiritual complacency mirror the concerns of *James* 1:6-8 and *Revelation* 3:1-3, revealing how the earliest assemblies understood the dangers of wavering faith.

Additional Ancient Writings Supporting *Shepherd Of Hermas'* Themes:

- *1 and 2 Clement* (repentance, unity, moral renewal, endurance under pressure)

- *Didache* (Two Ways tradition, ethical instruction, community discipline)
- *Testaments of the Twelve Patriarchs* (moral purity, repentance, angelic oversight)
- *Jubilees* (covenantal obedience, angelic mediation, moral accountability)
- *Ezekiel* and *Hosea* (repentance, restoration, new heart, covenant renewal)
- *Zechariah* (purification, cleansing, divine discipline)
- *1 Enoch* (angelic oversight, judgment, moral testing)
- *2 Baruch* and *4 Ezra* (repentance, divine justice, perseverance under trial)
- *Apocryphon of Abraham* (heavenly visions, moral discernment, divine judgment)

New Testament Writings Resonating With Themes Within *Shepherd Of Hermas*:

- *Matthew* 13 (parables of growth, judgment, and moral discernment)
- *Luke* 15 (repentance, restoration, divine mercy)
- *John* 15 (vine and branches, fruitfulness, discipline)
- *Acts* 3:19 (repentance leading to times of refreshing)
- *Romans* 12:1-2 (transformation through renewal)
- *1 Corinthians* 3:9-17 (living stones, testing, purification)
- *Galatians* 5:22-23 (fruit of the Spirit)
- *James* 1:6-8, 21–27 (double-mindedness, purity, obedience)
- *1 Peter* 1:13-16; 2:4-5 (holiness, spiritual house)
- *Hebrews* 6:1-6; 12:5-11 (repentance, discipline, perseverance)
- *Revelation* 2–3 (warnings to assemblies, call to repentance, endurance)

✦✧✦

Ignatius Of Antioch

A Voice of Endurance and Apostolic Unity

"Be eager, therefore, to be firmly grounded in the teachings of the Lord and the apostles." – Ignatius of Antioch, To the Ephesians 11

"It is fitting, then, not only to be called Christians, but to be such." – Ignatius of Antioch, To the Magnesians 4

"Apart from Him we have no true life." – Ignatius of Antioch, To the Trallians 9

"It is the cross that is my only hope, and in it I find my resurrection." – Ignatius of Antioch, To the Romans 6

"Wherever the shepherd is, there follow as sheep." – Ignatius of Antioch, To the Philadelphians 2

"Wherever the shepherd is, there follow as sheep." – Ignatius of Antioch, To the Smyrnaeans 8

"Stand firm, like an anvil under the hammer." – Ignatius of Antioch, To Polycarp 3

Ignatius, the steadfast bishop of Antioch who carried the apostolic faith from the first generation into the age of persecution, left a witness whose clarity, courage, and prophetic depth shaped the conscience of the early assemblies.

1. Ignatius of Antioch

Ignatius is one of the most luminous witnesses of the generation immediately following the apostles. A disciple of both Peter and John, Ignatius carried within him the living message of those who had walked with יֵשׁוּעַ/Yeshua. His life reflects prophetic hope, apostolic teaching, and the suffering love of the Messiah.

Ancient testimony consistently presents Ignatius as a man formed by the apostles and entrusted with their teaching:

> *"Ignatius, the second bishop of Antioch after Peter, was a man of great zeal and courage." – Eusebius, Ecclesiastical History 3.22.1*
>
> *"Ignatius, who was also called Theophorus, succeeded Evodius as bishop of the church in Antioch." – Eusebius, Ecclesiastical History 3.36.2*
>
> *"Ignatius, the disciple of the apostles and the second bishop of Antioch, was condemned to the beasts for the testimony of Christ." – Jerome, Lives of Illustrious Men 16*

Ignatius' final journey to Rome undertaken with joy rather than fear became a living testimony that the kingdom of יהוה/*Yahweh* advances through the faithfulness of His people. Ignatius' life and words continue to bear fruit, reminding every generation that the path of the righteous is marked by love, unity, and endurance until the return of the Messiah.

2. Epistles of Ignatius

Ignatius' writings – known in their earliest Semitic form as *The Letters of Ignatius (Iggeretot Ignatyos)* – were composed on the road to his martyrdom in Rome. They reveal a shepherd urging unity, purity of teaching, and steadfastness among those who await the appearance of the King.

He wrote letters to assemblies in six different cities: the *Ephesians, Magnesians, Philadelphians, Romans, Smyrnaeans,* and the *Trallians*, and one additional personal letter to Polycarp, the bishop of the Smyrnaean assembly (which was also addressed in Revelation 2). Ignatius' seven letters strengthened the assemblies through exhortation, encouragement, and correction. His letter to Polycarp offered pastoral counsel, urging him to stand firm, shepherd wisely, and remain steadfast in trials – revealing the relational nature of early leadership among the followers of יֵשׁוּעַ/Yeshua.

Ignatius emphasizes the structure of the early assemblies, affirming the role of bishops, elders, and deacons as guardians of the apostolic commission. He defends the apostolic faith against false teachings, urging believers to remain rooted in what they had received from those who walked with יֵשׁוּעַ/Yeshua.

His letters echo the voice of John in their emphasis on love, truth, and discernment, and they reflect Peter's call to endure suffering with courage. Through them, Ignatius carries forward the memorial of apostolic teaching and the call to remain faithful.

3. Authentication Of Ignatius' Letters

The ancient testimony surrounding the writings of Ignatius affirms their authenticity and reveals how they were preserved within the assemblies' apostolic heritage. His letters were composed during his journey to martyrdom and treasured by the early church as faithful witnesses to the apostolic tradition.

> *"Ignatius has left us epistles which are full of instruction and of the soundest doctrine." – Eusebius, Ecclesiastical History 3.36.13 (early 4th century)*
>
> *"The epistles of Ignatius… are held in great honor." – Jerome, Lives of Illustrious Men 16 (late 4th century)*
>
> *"Ignatius… wrote letters which are of great profit to the Church." – Jerome, Letter 70.4 (late 4th century)*
>
> *"The blessed Ignatius… strengthened the churches by his letters, which preserve the true doctrine." – Theodoret, Dialogue III (mid-5th century)*

Ignatius saw the assemblies not as scattered groups but as one unified body – a people called to endure, remain faithful, and hold fast to the truth entrusted to them. His voice is not merely historical; it is prophetic. His journey to martyrdom mirrors the path of Daniel's companions, יֵשׁוּעַ/Yeshua the suffering Servant and Lamb of יהוה/Yahweh who overcame through obedience.

4. Edifying Value Of Ignatius' Writings For The Modern Reader

Seen through this lens, the content of Ignatius' writings reveals their enduring apostolic value and their contribution to the wider Scriptural witness. His letters offer a rare and precious glimpse into the life of the early assemblies – communities refined through trial, strengthened through unity, and anchored in the hope of the coming kingdom.

Ignatius' prophetic contribution is not a new revelation but a living embodiment of the prophetic arc: a witness that faithfulness unto death is the path of the righteous. His letters call believers to unity, purity of doctrine, and steadfast endurance, echoing the exhortations of יֵשׁוּעַ/Yeshua to the overcomers and the pastoral heart of John.

For modern readers, Ignatius remains a bridge between the apostles and the generations that followed. His voice still speaks with clarity: a shepherd urging faithfulness, a witness strengthening the assemblies, and a disciple carrying forward the memory of the apostles. Few writings offer a clearer window into the heart of the earliest believers than the words he left behind.

✦✧✦

TWO-FOLD WITNESS:
HOW IGNATIUS' WRITINGS AFFIRM AND
ARE AFFIRMED BY OTHER PROPHETIC WITNESSES

Essential Content From Ignatius Of Antioch's Writings That Confirm The Biblical Author's Declarations And Teachings:

- Unity under יְשׁוּעַ/Yeshua and the bishop illuminates early church order reflected in *Acts* and the pastoral New Testament epistles. Ignatius' insistence on one faith, one altar, and one shepherd echoes *Acts* 20:28, *1 Timothy* 3, and *Titus* 1, revealing how the earliest assemblies understood apostolic authority and communal harmony.
- The theology of martyrdom deepens the meaning of "take up your cross" (*Matthew* 16:24; *Revelation* 1:9; 2:10; 2:13; 6:9–11; 7:14; 11:7–10; 12:11; 13:7, 10, 15; 14:13; 16:6; 17:6; 18:24; 20:4).
- Ignatius' longing to imitate the Messiah in suffering parallels *Philippians* 1:20-21, *2 Timothy* 4:6-8, and the witness of *Revelation* 2:10, where faithfulness unto death becomes the highest form of discipleship.
- The imitation of Christ resonates with Paul's exhortations in *1 Corinthians* 11:1 and *Ephesians* 5:1-2.
- Ignatius' letters reveal a lived expression of this imitation – humility, endurance, sacrificial love, and unwavering loyalty to the Messiah.
- The reality of spiritual conflict aligns with *Ephesians* 6 and *Revelation*'s cosmic imagery.
- Ignatius speaks of unseen powers, deception, and the need for vigilance, echoing the apostolic worldview that the assemblies stand within a cosmic struggle between truth and falsehood, light and darkness.

Additional Ancient Writings Supporting Ignatius' Themes:

- *1 Enoch* (cosmic conflict, angelic oversight, judgment, and the vindication of the righteous)
- *2 Baruch* and *4 Ezra* (suffering of the righteous, divine justice, endurance)
- The *Didache* (community order, ethical formation, unity, and discernment of teachers)

- *Shepherd of Hermas* (repentance, purity, spiritual warfare, angelic guardianship)
- Polycarp (shared pastoral and martyrdom themes; continuity of apostolic teaching; emphasis on endurance, righteousness, and unity)
- Early martyrdom traditions (e.g., *Martyrdom of Polycarp*), which preserve the early church's understanding of faithful witness, spiritual conflict, and the hope of resurrection – paralleling *Revelation* 6:9-11 and *Hebrews* 11–12.

New Testament Writings Resonating With Ignatius' Pastoral And Martyrdom Themes:

- *Matthew* 10 and 16 (discipleship, suffering, taking up the cross)
- *Luke* 9 and 14 (cost of discipleship, loyalty to the Messiah)
- *John* 10 and 17 (unity under the Shepherd, oneness of the flock)
- *Acts* 20 (shepherding the flock, guarding against false teachers)
- *Romans* 8 (suffering, glory, spiritual conflict)
- *Philippians* 1–3 (imitation of Christ, suffering as participation in The Messiah's life)
- *1 Peter* 1–5 (endurance, holiness, shepherding, suffering for righteousness)
- *Revelation* 2–3 (faithfulness unto death, overcoming, spiritual vigilance)

———————— ✦✧✦ ————————

Polycarp Of Smyrna

The Eyewitness Disciple Of John

"He who endures to the end shall be saved." – Matthew 24:13

"Be watchful, stand firm in the faith, be courageous, be strong." – 1 Corinthians 16:13

"Let us run with all earnestness to attain the crown of righteousness." – 1 Clement 34

"I am God's (יהוה/Yahweh) wheat, and I am ground by the teeth of beasts that I may be found pure bread." – Ignatius, To The Romans 4

"Be faithful unto death, and I will give you the crown of life." – Revelation 2:10

"Stand fast, therefore, in this faith, and follow the example of the Lord." – Polycarp, Epistle to the Philippians 1.2

The writings attributed to Polycarp, bishop of Smyrna, situated within apostolic memory and shaped by apostolic memory, offer insight into steadfast faith, moral instruction, and the endurance of the early church.

1. Polycarp of Smyrna

Polycarp is one of the most beloved figures of the post-apostolic age. He was a disciple of the apostle John, a companion of Ignatius of Antioch, and a shepherd who carried forward the living memory of the apostles into the second century. Appointed as bishop of Smyrna, he embodied the continuity of the apostolic witness with humility, courage, and unwavering devotion to יֵשׁוּעַ/Yeshua.

Ancient writers consistently describe him as a man formed by apostolic teaching:

> *"Polycarp, who was appointed bishop of the Church in Smyrna by the apostles themselves, was a man of great dignity and steadfastness." – Eusebius, Ecclesiastical History 4.14.3*
>
> *"Polycarp, the disciple of the apostle John and the teacher of many in Asia, was eminent for his holiness and simplicity."–Jerome, Lives of Illustrious Men*

Polycarp maintained a close relationship with Ignatius of Antioch. Ignatius wrote to him personally, and Polycarp later preserved and circulated Ignatius' letters among the assemblies:

> *"Both you and Ignatius wrote to me, that if anyone should go to Syria he should carry your letter with him; and this I will attend to if I find a fitting opportunity, either I myself or one whom I shall send as a representative on your behalf. We send you, as you requested, the letters of Ignatius which he wrote to us, together with any others that we have in our possession, as many as we could find; these are appended to this letter." – Polycarp, Letter to the Philippians 13.1–13.2*

"As for Ignatius, and those who were with him, you have written to us that if anyone should go to Syria he should also carry your letters; and this we will do as you requested, as we have already sent you the letters of Ignatius which he wrote to us, and all the others which we had by us, as many as we could find." – Martyrdom of Polycarp 13.2

Through Polycarp, we see a living bridge between the New Testament era and the emerging assemblies of the second century – a shepherd who guarded the apostolic faith with integrity and love.

2. Writings By Or About Polycarp

Polycarp's surviving work, *Letter to the Philippians*, reveals a pastor deeply shaped by the Scriptures and the apostolic tradition. His letter displays familiarity with *Matthew, Luke, Acts, Romans, Corinthians, Galatians, Ephesians, Philippians, Thessalonians, Hebrews, 1 Peter*, and *1 John* – quoting or alluding to them with ease.

The letter emphasizes righteousness, humility, love, discernment, and steadfast endurance. Polycarp warns against false teachers and exhorts believers to remain faithful to the truth they had received. His pastoral tone reflects the heart of a shepherd who cared deeply for the spiritual well-being of the assemblies.

The believers in Smyrna also preserved *The Martyrdom of Polycarp*, one of the earliest Christian martyrdom accounts outside the New Testament. It records his arrest, trial, and execution with remarkable detail. When urged to deny יֵשׁוּעַ/Yeshua, Polycarp replied:

"Eighty and six years have I served Him, and He has done me no wrong; how then can I blaspheme my King who saved me?" – The Martyrdom of Polycarp 9

His death fulfilled the prophetic call given to the assembly to Smyrna in *Revelation* 2:8–11 – faithfulness unto death – and became a model of endurance for generations of believers.

Martyrdom of Polycarp

The Martyrdom of Polycarp is a completely separate work than his letter – composed not by Polycarp but by the assembly in Smyrna shortly after his death. It preserves an eyewitness account of his arrest, trial, and faithful martyrdom, and was circulated independently as an early Christian testimony to steadfast witness. Because both writings mention the letters of Ignatius, they are often printed together in collections of the Apostolic Fathers, but they remain distinct in authorship, purpose, and historical setting.

3. Authentication of Polycarp's Writings

The authenticity of *The Letter to the Philippians* is strongly affirmed by ancient testimony. Early Christian writers consistently recognized it as a genuine work of Polycarp and valued it for its apostolic fidelity.

"Polycarp… has left a letter which is of great value." – Eusebius, Ecclesiastical History 3.36.13

"Polycarp… wrote a very useful letter to the Philippians, which is still read in

the churches." – Jerome, Lives of Illustrious Men 17

"The epistle of Polycarp is most excellent and edifying, and it preserves the apostolic doctrine with great fidelity." – Theodoret of Cyrus, Dialogue III

The Smyrnaean community's preservation of *The Martyrdom of Polycarp* further demonstrates the esteem in which he was held. As one of the assemblies addressed by יְשׁוּעַ/Yeshua in *Revelation* 2:8–11, Smyrna understood suffering and endurance; Polycarp's life and death embodied the very message spoken to them.

These testimonies – literary, historical, and communal – provide a strong and early chain of authentication for Polycarp's letter and for the reliability of the traditions surrounding his life and martyrdom.

4. Edifying Value Of Polycarp's Writings For The Modern Reader

Polycarp stands at the threshold between the apostolic age and the emerging assemblies, offering a window into how the earliest believers understood covenantal faithfulness. His writings reveal a community shaped through Scripture, guided by apostolic memory, and sustained by the hope of the coming kingdom.

His exhortations echo the teachings of Paul, Peter, and John, showing how the apostolic voice continued to guide the assemblies long after the apostles had departed. Through Polycarp, we see how Scripture was shared, read, applied, and lived within communities facing pressure, persecution, and doctrinal confusion.

His martyrdom carries forward the prophetic theme of faithfulness unto death as יְשׁוּעַ/Yeshua told the Smyrnaean assembly in *Revelation* 2, reminding every generation that the path of the faithful is marked by steadfast devotion to the Messiah. His life and letter continue to call believers to endurance, purity, unity, love, discernment, and unwavering trust in יְשׁוּעַ/Yeshua.

Polycarp's witness remains a living testimony that the faith once delivered to the saints was not only remembered but embodied, guarded, and passed on with integrity and courage.

✦✧✦

TWO-FOLD WITNESS:
HOW POLYCARP'S WRITINGS AFFIRM AND
ARE AFFIRMED BY OTHER PROPHETIC WITNESSES

Essential Content From Polycarp's Writings And Legacy Clarifying The Biblical Author's Declarations And Teachings:

- *The Letter of Polycarp* preserves apostolic ethical instruction, illuminating the continuity between Paul's teachings and the early practice of the followers of יֵשׁוּעַ/Yeshua. Its exhortations toward righteousness, endurance, humility, and love echo *Philippians, 1 Thessalonians, 1 Peter*, and the New Testament's pastoral epistles, revealing how the earliest assemblies lived out the apostolic commands.
- *The Martyrdom of Polycarp* provides a vivid example of faithful witness, clarifying New Testament themes of perseverance and suffering for Christ. Polycarp's calm courage, prophetic composure, and willingness to "be faithful unto death" resonate with *Revelation* 2:10, *Hebrews* 11–12, and *Matthew* 10:28.
- Ignatius' *Letter to Polycarp* reveals early pastoral relationships and the transmission of apostolic authority. Its correspondence demonstrates how the earliest bishops encouraged one another, guarded the flock, and preserved the teachings handed down from the apostles, echoing *Acts* 20:28-32 and *2 Timothy* 2:2.
- Early church tradition preserves Polycarp as a direct disciple of John, reinforcing the continuity of apostolic remembrance. His testimony bridges the apostolic age and the generations that followed, confirming the teachings of *1, 2* and *3 John* regarding love, truth, discernment, and perseverance.

Additional Ancient Writings Supporting Themes Of This Chapter:

- Irenaeus' *Against Heresies* (Polycarp's testimony, apostolic memory, and the preservation of the rule of faith; firsthand witness to Polycarp's teaching and character)
- The *Didache* (ethical parallels, community order, Two Ways tradition, and early church discipline)
- *Shepherd of Hermas* (repentance, purity, perseverance, angelic oversight)
- *1 Clement* (unity, humility, endurance, apostolic order)

- *Letters of Ignatius* (martyrdom, imitation of Christ, pastoral exhortation)
- *Testaments of the Twelve Patriarchs* (ethical formation, covenantal faithfulness and righteousness)

New Testament Writings Resonating With Polycarp's Ethical And Pastoral Themes:

- *Matthew* 5–7 (ethical instruction, righteousness, purity of heart)
- *Matthew* 10 and 16 (discipleship, suffering, taking up the cross)
- *John* 13–17 (love, unity, obedience, perseverance)
- *Acts* 20 (shepherding the flock, guarding against false teachers)
- *Romans* 12–15 (ethical formation, humility, love, endurance)
- *1 Corinthians* 13–16 (love, resurrection hope, steadfastness)
- *1 Peter* 1–5 (suffering for righteousness, holiness, shepherding)
- *Revelation* 2–3 (faithfulness unto death, overcoming, discernment)

Irenaeus Of Lyons

The Defender of Apostolic Tradition Against Rising Heresies

"We have learned the plan of our salvation from those to whom the apostles entrusted the churches." – Irenaeus, Against Heresies 3.3.1.

"Irenaeus, who was a disciple of Polycarp, and through him of the apostles, delivered the tradition of the true faith as he had received it."
– Eusebius, Ecclesiastical History 5.20

"Irenaeus, the disciple of Polycarp and the witness of apostolic doctrine, wrote many works in which he preserved the ancient faith."
– Jerome, On Illustrious Men 35

"Irenaeus, being a man of the apostolic times, preserved the doctrine he had received from the elders and delivered it without corruption."
– Epiphanius, Panarion 31.9

"The blessed Irenaeus, successor of the apostles, handed down the preaching of the truth as he had learned it from the ancients."
– Rufinus, Ecclesiastical History 5.8

The writings of Irenaeus of Lyons, demonstrates that Irenaeus was a defender of the early faith handed down by the apostles, situated within the second-century church offer insight into apostolic instruction, theological clarity, and the unity of Scripture.

1. Irenaeus of Lyons As An Author

Irenaeus is one of the most significant voices of the post-apostolic age – a disciple of Polycarp, who himself had been taught by the apostle John. Through this living chain of memory, Irenaeus carried forward the apostolic proclamation into the late second century with clarity, pastoral concern, and unwavering devotion to the truth.

Ancient witnesses consistently describe him as a man formed by apostolic teaching and entrusted with the preservation of the "rule of faith":

> *"Irenaeus, whose name means 'peaceable,' was well suited to his character… He wrote many letters in which he exhorted and admonished the brethren, and he was well known as a man of sound judgment." – Eusebius, Ecclesiastical History 5.8.4*

> *"These things are stated by Irenaeus… He also testifies that he had himself seen Polycarp in his early youth." – Eusebius, Ecclesiastical History 5.20.4*

> *"Irenaeus, a man of apostolic times and of approved faith, has handed down the rule of truth in his writings." – Rufinus of Aquileia, Preface to Origen's Commentary on Romans*

> *"Irenaeus, the disciple of Polycarp and the witness of apostolic doctrine, was illustrious in all virtues." – Jerome, Lives of Illustrious Men 35*

Born in Asia Minor and later serving as presbyter and then bishop in Lyons (Gaul), Irenaeus ministered in a time of doctrinal confusion and rising Gnostic distortions. His pastoral heart, combined with his theological clarity, made him a steadying presence for the assemblies. Through him, the apostolic proclamation was not only preserved but articulated with a depth that shaped Christian thought for centuries.

2. Irenaeus' Writings

Irenaeus' most influential work is his five-volume treatise *Against Heresies (Adversus Haereses)*, a comprehensive refutation of Gnostic teachings and a robust exposition of the apostolic faith. In this work, he sets forth the unity of Scripture, the continuity of the covenants, the centrality of the incarnation, the goodness of creation, and the apostolic "rule of truth", and the identity of יֵשׁוּעַ/Yeshua as the incarnate Son. Eusebius summarizes the work succinctly:

> *"Irenaeus has left us a most complete refutation of the heretics of his time, entitled*

> *Against Heresies. In this work he sets forth the apostolic preaching and the tradition of the truth which he had received." – Eusebius, Ecclesiastical History 5.26.1*

In addition to *Against Heresies*, Irenaeus wrote other treatises, including a work *On the Ogdoad*, and numerous pastoral letters now lost but remembered by ancient witnesses.

His writings reveal a mind steeped in Scripture and a heart committed to the unity and purity of the assemblies. He writes not as a speculative philosopher but as a shepherd guarding the flock from teachings that threatened to sever believers from the apostolic proclamation.

3. Authenticity of Irenaeus' Writings

The authenticity of Irenaeus' writings is affirmed by a strong and early chain of testimony. Ancient authors consistently recognized his works as genuine and valued them for their fidelity to apostolic teaching.

> *"Irenaeus… wrote five books Against Heresies, in which he exposed the wicked doctrines of the Gnostics… He flourished in the reign of Commodus." – Jerome, Lives of Illustrious Men 35*
>
> *"Irenaeus, who was near to the apostolic age, is a faithful witness of the ancient doctrine." – Jerome, Letter 33.4*
>
> *"The blessed Irenaeus refutes these errors at length in his writings, preserving the apostolic teaching without deviation." – Epiphanius, Panarion 33.3.7*
>
> *"Irenaeus… has exposed the madness of the Gnostics in his renowned books." – Theodoret, Compendium of Heretical Fables 1.24*

These testimonies from other witnesses – spanning the 4th and 5th centuries – demonstrate that Irenaeus' writings were widely known, circulated, and trusted as authoritative expositions of the apostolic faith. His historical proximity to Polycarp, and thus to the apostolic generation, further strengthens the reliability of his witness.

The historical evidence is so substantial that modern readers are compelled to take Irenaeus seriously as a guardian of early Christian memory and doctrine.

4. Edifying Value Of Irenaeus' Writings For The Modern Reader

Viewed through this authenticating lens, the writings of Irenaeus hold significant value for believers in every generation. His work stands at the crossroads of Scripture, apostolic memory, and the emerging theological identity of the early assemblies. He shows how the earliest followers of יְשׁוּעַ/Yeshua understood the unity of the biblical narrative and how they resisted distortions that threatened to fracture the faith.

For contemporary readers, Irenaeus provides a model of how to read Scripture as one unified story, a reminder that doctrine is rooted in the lived memory of the apostles, a vision of covenantal faithfulness grounded in righteousness and truth, and a pastoral voice calling believers to discernment, unity, and endurance.

Irenaeus' writings continue to strengthen the vine of יְשׁוּעַ/Yeshua by keeping believers rooted in the apostolic proclamation. Through Irenaeus, we see how the faith once delivered to the saints was preserved, defended, and passed on with clarity and conviction – bearing fruit for generations.

———— ✦✧✦ ————

TWO-FOLD WITNESS:
HOW IRENAEUS' WRITINGS AFFIRM AND ARE AFFIRMED BY OTHER PROPHETIC WITNESSES

Essential Content From Irenaeus' Writings That Clarify The Biblical Authors' Declarations And Teachings:

- Irenaeus preserves the earliest comprehensive defense of apostolic teaching, clarifying the continuity between the apostles and the second-century assemblies. His *Against Heresies* demonstrates how the early church safeguarded the apostolic proclamation, echoing the concerns of *Acts* 20:28-32, *2 Timothy 1–2,* and *Jude.*
- His doctrine of recapitulation illuminates Paul's teaching on Adam, Christ, and the restoration of humanity. Irenaeus' vision of the Messiah "summing up" all things in Himself parallels *Romans* 5,
- *1 Corinthians* 15, and *Ephesians* 1:10, revealing how the early church understood the cosmic scope of redemption.
- Irenaeus' reliance on the fourfold Gospel tradition clarifies early apostolic views of Scripture and canon. His affirmation of *Matthew, Mark, Luke,* and *John* as the Spirit-given witness to the Messiah reflects the canonical consciousness already present in *Luke 1:1*-4 and *2 Peter* 1:16-21 and shows how the earliest believers recognized the unity of the Gospel proclamation.
- Irenaeus' testimony about Polycarp and John preserves the chain of apostolic remembrance central to this era. Irenaeus' firsthand memories of Polycarp and his direct connection to the apostle John anchor the transmission of teaching described in *2 Timothy* 2:2 and confirm the living continuity of the apostolic voice.

Additional Ancient Writings Supporting Irenaeus' Themes:

- *1 Enoch* (Son of Man imagery, judgment, resurrection, cosmic renewal)
- *Testaments of the Twelve Patriarchs* (messianic expectation, moral
- exhortation)
- *2 Baruch* and *4 Ezra* (prophetic continuity, divine justice, restoration)
- *Didache* (ethical formation, community order, apostolic teaching)
- *Shepherd of Hermas* (repentance, purity, divine discipline, angelic oversight)

- Justin Martyr (parallel defenses of apostolic faith, Logos theology, messianic fulfillment, and the continuity between Israel's Scriptures and the Gospel)
- Papias (early traditions about the apostles, Gospel origins, oral transmission, and the preservation of eyewitness memory)

New Testament Writings That Resonate With Irenaeus' Theological And Pastoral Themes:

- *Matthew* 24–25 (judgment, fulfillment, messianic authority)
- *Luke 1–4* (prophetic continuity, fulfillment in the Messiah)
- *John* 1–5 (incarnation, divine Sonship, life in the Word)
- *Acts* 1–3 (apostolic witness, prophetic fulfillment, restoration)
- *Romans* 5–8 (Adam and Christ, new creation, life in the Spirit)
- *1 Corinthians* 15 (resurrection, new humanity, victory over death)
- *Ephesians* 1–3 (recapitulation, divine economy, unity in Christ)
- *1 John* (truth, love, discernment, apostolic testimony)
- *Revelation* 1–5 (the Lamb, divine authority, heavenly witness)

SEVENTH ERA: The Ancient Path To The End Of The Age

Following the Ancient Path in the Last Days

Hearing יהוה/Yahweh's Voice From The Beginning, Embracing The Wider Witness, And Walking In The Light Of All His Words

"Blessed are all who walk in the way of righteousness, who hear the words of wisdom and do not turn aside." – 1 Enoch 99:10

"And all their generations shall know that I have not abandoned them, for my words remain with them as a witness forever." – Jubilees 1:25

"Stand at the crossroads and look; ask for the ancient paths, where the good way is, and walk in it, and you will find rest for your souls." – Jeremiah 6:16

"One generation shall praise thy works to another and shall declare thy mighty acts." – Psalm 145:4

"Wisdom pours herself out like water before the sons of men, and her glory is not cut off from generation to generation." – Ecclesiasticus/Sirach 24:31

"For the righteous have the ancient paths in their hearts, and they understand the ways of the Most High." – 2 Baruch 85:3

"The works of God (יהוה/Yahweh) are known from of old, and His words endure forever." – 1 Clement 27:3

From the beginning, יהוה/Yahweh has called His people to hear His words of wisdom and not turn aside, as the righteous who "*walk in the way of righteousness*" (*1 Enoch* 99:10) and listen when Wisdom pours herself out before the sons of men (*Ecclesiasticus/Sirach*□24:31). His voice has never fallen silent, for He declared that His words would "*remain with them as a witness forever*" (*Jubilees*□1:25), carried from age to age as one generation praises His works to another (*Psalm*□145:4). Those who embrace this preserved witness stand at the crossroads and look for the ancient paths (*Jeremiah*□6:16), receiving the Good Way handed down through the prophets, the sages, and the faithful who recorded His mighty acts. And those who truly receive His words walk in them, finding rest for their souls, for "*the righteous have the ancient paths in their hearts*" (*2*□*Baruch*□85:3) and understand the ways of the Most High, knowing that "*the works of God are known from of old, and His words endure forever*" (*1*□*Clement*□27:3). In this unbroken testimony, the call to hear, to embrace, and to walk becomes the path of every generation.

Through prophets, scribes, and elders, יהוה/Yahweh entrusted His words to His servants, directing prophets to speak and moving those who recorded and preserved them for humanity. In the fullness of time, יֵשׁוּעַ/Yeshua completed this prophetic path by becoming the everlasting High Priest and the promised King whose Kingdom will never end (*Revelation* 1:5–6). His apostles, taught by Him and empowered by the Spirit, carried forward the same fulfillment, grounding their witness in the Scriptures. Later interpreters sought to show how the Law, the Prophets, the Psalms, and the Gospel formed one coherent narrative centered in יֵשׁוּעַ/Yeshua. Taken together, these voices form a single testimony entrusted to future generations.

Beginning in the 4th century, influential bishops and regional councils increasingly rejected or marginalized writings that did not fit within the developing canon. Earlier assemblies of יֵשׁוּעַ/Yeshua's followers read a wide range of edifying texts freely – such as *Shepherd of Hermas, Epistle/Teachings of Barnabas, 1 Clement*, Ignatius' *Epistles/Letters* and the *Didache* – but from the 4th century onward, church authorities restricted these works, treating them as *outside* the approved, authorized and official list of Scriptures. This shift is visible in Athanasius' *Festal Letter* of 367, which forbids the public reading of several long-valued books, and in the councils of Hippo (393) and Carthage (397/419), which formalized narrower canonical lists.

Each person must walk according to the measure of light they are willing to receive. Scripture repeatedly affirms that every word spoken by יהוה/Yahweh through His servants the prophets (2 *Kings* 17:13; *Ezra* 9:11; *Jeremiah* 7:25; *Daniel* 9:6; *Amos* 3:7; *Zechariah* 1:6; *Revelation* 10:7; 11:18; 22:6) and all of His Words stand as a witness for all generations. His people are accountable for how they respond to The Good Shepherd's voice.

> *"I am the good shepherd: the good shepherd giveth his life for the sheep."; "I am the good shepherd, and know my sheep, and am known of mine." "And other sheep I have, which are not of this fold: them also I must bring, and they shall hear my voice; and there shall be one fold, and one shepherd." – John 10:11, 14, 16*
>
> *"And I will set up one shepherd over them, and he shall feed them, even my servant David; he shall feed them, and he shall be their shepherd." – Ezekiel 34:23*
>
> *"And David my servant shall be king over them; and they all shall have one shepherd." – Ezekiel 37:24*
>
> *"Woe be unto the pastors that destroy and scatter the sheep of my pasture! saith the Lord." – Jeremiah 23:1*
>
> *"And I will set up shepherds over them which shall feed them: and they shall fear no more, nor be dismayed, neither shall they be lacking, saith the Lord." – Jeremiah 23:4*
>
> *"Behold, the days come, saith the Lord, that I will raise unto David a righteous Branch, and a King shall reign and prosper, and shall execute judgment and justice in the earth." – Jeremiah 23:5*
>
> *"Now the God of peace, that brought again from the dead our Lord Jesus, that great shepherd of the sheep, through the blood of the everlasting covenant, Make you perfect in every good work to do his will, working in you that which is wellpleasing in his sight..." – Hebrews 13:20-21*

The question is never merely whether a text was preserved within a particular collection or bound in a specific codex, but whether it bears the true Testimony of the One who speaks from heaven.

In the end, every disciple will give account for how they managed what He revealed – whether they welcomed His words, ignored them, or treated lightly what He entrusted to His appointed faithful and righteous "servants – His prophets ("servants the prophets" – Revelation 10:7; 11:18; 22:6). Such a truth invites humility, reflection, and a willingness to listen wherever His voice is found.

Reading the Wider Witness Without Fear

Modern believers have inherited caution around ancient writings outside the canon, yet the earliest generations did not share this fear. Early believers did not divide the world into "safe" and "unsafe" writings. They listened for the voice that had spoken from the beginning. They read these writings because the prophets gave them, the apostles quoted and encouraged them, and the early assemblies received and preserved them. Early believers read these ancient Hebrew prophetic writings to understand Scripture more fully.

- יהוה/Yahweh has spoken.
- The story has been told.
- The witnesses have written.
- The words have been preserved and passed down.

Generations have passed before us. We have searched, found, and read all the words we could find of what יהוה/*Yahweh* spoke. As readers go forward, may the awareness of these preserved words lead them to seek them out, learn from them, and walk in the light they offer.

AFTER MATTER

Recommended Reading Lists

A Curated Though Not Exhaustive List Of The Most Notable Ancient Jewish Texts And Writings From Well-Known Prophets, The Apostles, Early-Centuries Bishops, And Faithful Followers of יֵשׁוּעַ/Yeshua

Ancient Hebrew Writings:

- 1 Enoch
- Jubilees
- Jasher
- Testament of Abraham
- Testament of Isaac
- Testament of Jacob (Israel)
- Testaments of the Twelve Patriarchs
- Apocalypse/Apocryphon of Abraham
- 1 and 2 Baruch
- 1 Esdras /4 Ezra & 2 Esdras)
- Psalms of Solomon
- Wisdom of Solomon
- Sirach (Ecclesiasticus)
- 1-2 and 4 Maccabees
- Book of Gad the Seer
- Vision/Ascension of Isaiah
- Selected Dead Sea Scrolls texts and fragments

*** There are many other excellent extracanonical texts which were not featured in this book.

Apostolic Writings Associated With The Apostles

- The Didache
- Acts of the Apostles
- Protoevangelium of James
- History of Joseph the Carpenter
- Epistle of Barnabas
- Gospel of Nicodemus/Acts of Pilate
- Letters of Ignatius of Antioch
- Epistle of Polycarp to the Philippians
- 1 and 2 Clement
- Against Heresies by Irenaeus of Lyons
- The Shepherd of Hermas

———— ✦✧✦ ————

Writings of Later Witnesses (Optional)

- Antiquities of the Jews (Josephus)
- Dialogue with Trypho (Justin Martyr)
- Fragments of Irenaeus (Against Heresies)
- On Baptism (Tertullian)
- Against Marcion (Tertullian)
- Commentary on John (Origen)
- Ecclesiastical History (Eusebius)
- Panarion (Epiphanius)
- Commentaries on the Prophets (Jerome)
- City of God (Augustine)

✦✧✦

Recommended Sources For Ancient Texts

These print collections and open-access archives provide reliable access to the ancient Jewish and early Hebrew writings preserved among the followers of יֵשׁוּעַ/Yeshua referenced throughout this book.

Print Collections

- ***Ante-Nicene Fathers / Nicene and Post-Nicene Fathers* (Schaff Series)** Extensive collections of early Hebrew authors among the followers of יֵשׁוּעַ/Yeshua, including Justin Martyr, Tertullian, Origen, Eusebius, Jerome, and Augustine.
- ***The Apocrypha and Pseudepigrapha of the Old Testament* (ed. R. H. Charles)** A classic two-volume set offering older but still valuable translations of many post-exilic works.
- ***The Apostolic Fathers* (Loeb or Penguin Classics)** Early Hebrew writings preserved among the followers of יֵשׁוּעַ/Yeshua, such as *1 Clement, Ignatius, Polycarp, Didache*, and *Shepherd of Hermas.*
- ***The Complete 100-Book Apocrypha* (Expanded 2024 Edition, LSV)** A broad anthology containing all major post-exilic and early Hebrew texts preserved among the followers of יֵשׁוּעַ/Yeshua and cited in this book.
- ***The Dead Sea Scrolls: A New Translation* (Wise, Abegg, Cook)** A readable translation of major Qumran texts, including sectarian writings and fragments of *1 Enoch* and *Jubilees.*
- ***The Old Testament Pseudepigrapha*, Vols. 1–2 (ed. James H. Charlesworth)** The standard scholarly collection of Jewish pseudepigraphal writings with introductions and modern translations.

Free Online Sources

- **British Library Digitized Manuscripts** (www.bl.uk/manuscripts) High quality scans of ancient codices, biblical manuscripts, and early Christian writings.
- **Center for the Study of New Testament Manuscripts (CSNTM)** (www.csntm.org) High resolution images of early New Testament manuscripts used among the earliest followers of יֵשׁוּעַ/Yeshua.
- **Christian Classics Ethereal Library (CCEL)** (www.ccel.org) Free patristic writings, including early commentaries and preserved teachings from the earliest assemblies.
- **Dead Sea Scrolls Digital Library (Israel Antiquities Authority)** (www.deadseascrolls.org.il) High resolution images and transcriptions of Qumran manuscripts, including biblical and extracanonical scrolls.
- **Digital Dead Sea Scrolls (Israel Museum, Shrine of the Book)** (www.imj.org.il) Fully digitized scrolls with zoomable images and curated explanations for readers.
- **Early Christian Writings** (www.earlychristianwritings.com) Open access translations of the Apostolic Fathers and early authors preserved among the followers of יֵשׁוּעַ/Yeshua.
- **Early Jewish Writings** (www.earlyjewishwritings.com) Public domain translations and introductions to Jewish texts from the Second Temple period.
- **HebrewGospels.com** (www.hebrewgospels.com) A free online project providing the Hebrew text and English translation of the Gospels, *Revelation*, *James*, and *Jude*, along with research tools, linguistic notes, and manuscript resources highlighting the Hebrew foundations of early New Testament writings.
- **Internet Archive** (www.archive.org) A vast digital repository of ancient manuscripts, facsimiles, codices, and historical texts relevant to Jewish, Hebraic, and early Christian traditions.

- **Leon Levy Dead Sea Scrolls Digital Library** (www.deadseascrolls.org.il) Featured-scrolls, enhanced imaging and searchable access to a wide range of Dead Sea Scroll fragments.
- **The Internet Sacred Text Archive** (www.sacred-texts.com) An enormous collection of public domain translations of post-exilic Jewish and early Hebrew writings.
- **The Online Critical Pseudepigrapha (OCP)** (www.ocp.tyndale.ca) Public domain translations and critical texts of *1□Enoch, Jubilees, the Testaments, Psalms of Solomon*, and related Second Temple writings.
- **Vatican Library Digital Collections** (www.digi.vatlib.it) Digitized manuscripts, early biblical codices, and historical works from Jewish and Christian antiquity.

Glossary

APOCRYPHA – A group of Jewish writings included in the ancient Greek Scriptures (the Septuagint) and used by early believers. These books provide historical and theological context for the world of יֵשׁוּעַ/Yeshua and the apostles, though later excluded from the Hebrew canon.

APOCRYPHA (1611 KJV) – The collection of fourteen writings placed between the Old and New Testaments in the original 1611 King James Bible. These books include *1 and 2 Esdras, Tobit, Judith,* Additions to *Esther, Wisdom of Solomon, Ecclesiasticus (Sirach), Baruch, Letter of Jeremiah, Prayer of Azariah, Susanna, Bel and the Dragon, Prayer of Manasseh, 1 & 2 Maccabees.* They reflect the spiritual and historical world of post-exilic Judaism and were widely read in the early assemblies.

APOSTOLIC WITNESS – The living testimony handed down from the apostles through those who heard, remembered, and preserved their teaching within the earliest assemblies.

ASSEMBLY (EKKLESIA) – A gathered community of believers called together by יהוה/*Yahweh*; not a building, but a people shaped by covenant identity in every ERA.

CANON – A boundary drawn by later communities to identify a specific collection of writings. Canon reflects historical decisions, not the full scope of inspired or authoritative Scripture known across the ERAs.

COVENANT – יהוה/*YAHWEH*'s binding promise to His people, expressed through faithfulness, mercy, and generational continuity. Covenant identity shapes every era of the Biblical story. In Hebrew, "righteousness" (צדקה) is a relational term, describing covenant faithfulness lived out in loyalty to יהוה/*Yahweh*.

DEAD SEA SCROLLS – Ancient manuscripts discovered near Qumran, including Biblical books, commentaries, and community writings. They provide the earliest known copies of many Scriptures and reveal the interpretive world of early Judaism.

DIASPORA – Communities of Israelites or Jews living outside the land of Israel, formed through exile, displacement, or migration, who maintained a shared identity, Scripture, and covenant life while dwelling among foreign nations.

ECHAD אֶחָד – pronounced *eh-KHAD*, Meaning: "one," "unity", "one among many," or "first in sequence." A foundational Hebrew term expressing both singularity and unified plurality, depending on context. Used throughout Scripture to describe numerical oneness, covenantal unity, and collective harmony. In the Shema (*Deuteronomy* 6:4), *echad* affirms the unique, incomparable oneness of יהוה/*Yahweh*. The term can denote a compound unity (e.g., "one flesh" in *Genesis* 2:24) or a singular, exclusive one (e.g., "one day" in *Genesis* 1:5). Its feminine form is אַחַת (achat). (*Genesis* 1:5; 2:24; *Deuteronomy* 6:4).

ELECT – Those chosen by יהוה/*Yahweh* for covenant faithfulness and future inheritance. A term used across prophetic, apostolic, and extracanonical writings.

ESCHATOLOGY – The study or revelation of the final acts of יהוה/*Yahweh*'s redemptive plan. Eschatology concerns the culmination of history – judgment, resurrection, restoration, and the reign of Messiah.

EXTRACANONICAL WRITINGS – Texts valued, preserved, or referenced by believers across the ERAs that were not included in later canonical lists. These writings form part of the ancient library of memory.

HADES / SHEOL – The realm of the dead; the unseen place into which the Messiah descended in victory. In earlier ERAs, Sheol was the common term; later Greek-speaking assemblies used Hades.

MANDATE – A moral instruction or command given for shaping a holy life. Used especially in The *Shepherd of Hermas*, a text read widely in the early assemblies.

MASORETIC TEXT (MT) – The authoritative Hebrew text of the Jewish Scriptures compiled by the Masoretes over a 300-year period – between the 8th and 11th centuries CE. It forms the basis of most modern Old Testament translations.

MESSIAH – The anointed king promised in the Scriptures, expected to restore Israel, judge the nations, and reign in righteousness. In the New Testament, יֵשׁוּעַ/Yeshua is proclaimed as the fulfillment of this hope.

PARABLE – A narrative analogy that conveys spiritual or moral truth through story. Parables use familiar scenes to reveal deeper realities, often separating the discerning from the indifferent.

PROPHECY – A divine message revealed by the Spirit of יהוה/*Yahweh* concerning His will, His works, or His future purposes. Prophecy includes both the declaration of יהוה/*Yahweh*'s truth and the unveiling of what is to come.

PROPHETIC TRADITION – The unbroken line of voices – from Enoch to *John* – who spoke יהוה/*Yahweh* 's word and revealed His purposes. This tradition spans all ERAs and includes both canonical and extracanonical writings.

PSEUDEPIGRAPHA – Etymology: It is derived from Modern Latin, utilizing the Greek neuter plural of pseudepigraphos ("falsely inscribed" or "bearing a false title"). Early Usage: The term was used in the 1620s to describe books of false authorship, specifically those professing to be Biblical in character. Pseudepigrapha – the word first used among theologians in the early 17th century to place all ancient Christian writings not considered canonical Scripture into a category of false teaching. The word itself means "falsely inscribed" or "bearing a false title". Today It is commonly used to brand any writing outside the 66-book canon as a false or fabricated writing.

QUMRAN – The Judean wilderness site associated with the Dead Sea Scrolls. The writings found there preserve ancient Biblical manuscripts and early Jewish interpretations that illuminate the beliefs of various groups in the 1st century.

REMNANT – The faithful portion of Israel preserved by יהוה/*Yahweh* across the ERAs, through whom His covenant purposes continue.

RESURRECTION – The raising of the dead in glory; the central hope of Israel and the early assemblies. Resurrection is the promised renewal of creation and humanity.

REVELATION – "*Revelation*" (Capitalized and *italicized*) refers to the final prophetic book given to John. "revelation" (lowercase) refers to יהוה/*Yahweh*'s act of unveiling truth to His servants throughout history. One is a specific text; the other is the ongoing divine work that shaped the prophets and apostles.

RIGHTEOUSNESS – Right relationship with יהוה/*Yahweh*, expressed through justice, mercy, humility, and covenantal faithfulness. A defining virtue across all eras and generations.

SCRIBE – A trained writer or recorder of sacred instruction. In several ERAs, scribes preserved prophecy, covenant law, and apostolic teaching.

SEPTUAGINT (LXX) – The ancient Greek translation of the Hebrew Scriptures widely used in the time of יֵשׁוּעַ/Yeshua and the apostles. Most Old Testament quotations in the New Testament follow the Septuagint rather than the later Masoretic Text.

SHEMA – The central confession of Israel's faith: "Hear, O Israel: the LORD יהוה/*Yahweh* our God (אֱלֹהֵינוּ – Eloheinu), the LORD (יהוה – Yahweh) is one." (אֵל – 'El: root; אֱלוֹהַּ – Eloah: singular; אֱלֹהִים – Elohim: majestic plural; אֱלֹהֵינוּ – Eloheinu: "our God"). It affirms the unity and uniqueness of יהוה/*Yahweh* and anchors the covenant identity of Israel.

SIMILITUDE – A symbolic likeness or representative image used to reveal a truth through comparison. Similitudes appear in prophetic and apocalyptic writings, where heavenly realities are shown through earthly forms.

TETRAGRAMMATON – The four-letter covenant Name of the Almighty יהוה/*Yahweh*, revealed to Moses and preserved across the ERAs as the personal Name of the One who is, who was, and who will be.

THE AGE TO COME – The promised future era of renewal, resurrection, and the reign of the messiah.

PRESENT AGE – The current ERA *mark*ed by struggle, testing, and the call to faithfulness before the arrival of the Age to Come.

THE VINE – A Biblical image for the people of יהוה/*Yahweh*, rooted in Him and bearing fruit across generations and ERAs.

THE WAY – An early name for the path of discipleship and the life shaped by the teachings of יֵשׁוּעַ/Yeshua used by the earliest assemblies before later labels emerged.

WITNESS –A person or writing that testifies to the works, identity, or teachings of יהוה/*Yahweh* and His Messiah. Witnesses appear across all eras of the Biblical story.

www.ingramcontent.com/pod-product-compliance
Lightning Source LLC
LaVergne TN
LVHW040220110826
845146LV00005B/1348
* 9 7 9 8 9 9 5 2 8 5 9 0 8 *